S0-BLE-352

PiLLOW MOUNTAiN

Words
that
collaborate
with my
secret
heart
are
like
soil
that
accepts
the imprints
of
my
feet...
are
like
sand
that dallies
with my
toes...
are
like
wings
that
lend
themselves
to the
flight
of
my
spirit.

PiLLOW MOUNTAiN
Notes On Inhabiting
A Living Planet
by
Michael Bridge

Times Change PRESS

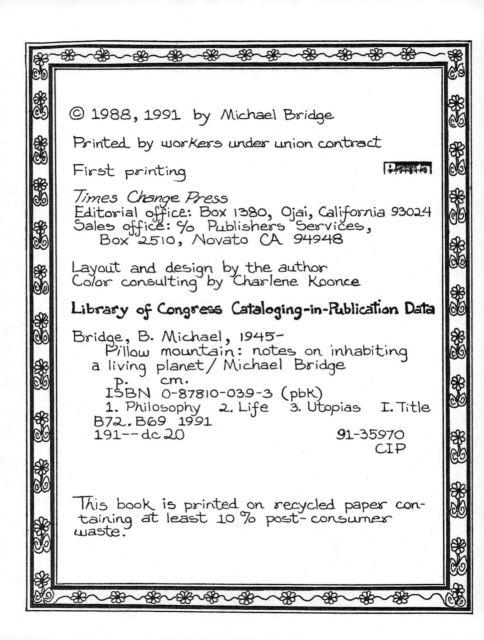

© 1988, 1991 by Michael Bridge

Printed by workers under union contract

First printing

Times Change Press
Editorial office: Box 1380, Ojai, California 93024
Sales office: % Publishers Services,
   Box 2510, Novato CA 94948

Layout and design by the author
Color consulting by Charlene Koonce

Library of Congress Cataloging-in-Publication Data

Bridge, B. Michael, 1945-
   Pillow mountain: notes on inhabiting
a living planet / Michael Bridge
      p.   cm.
   ISBN 0-87810-039-3 (pbk)
   1. Philosophy   2. Life   3. Utopias   I. Title
B72.B69 1991
191--dc20   91-35970
                                      CIP

This book is printed on recycled paper con-
taining at least 10% post-consumer
waste.

For the critters, all of them. We are not their masters. Faces of God...all.

THANK YOU SILENCE FOR MAKING A PLACE WHERE WORDS CAN LIVE. THANK YOU WORDS FOR MAKING A WAY FOR HEARTS TO SPEAK. THANK YOU SKY FOR FLYING AND EARTH FOR LANDING. THANK YOU TREES AND LEAVES AND BLADES OF GRASS FOR PRODUCING OXYGEN AND FOR CATCHING THE WIND LIKE STAUNCH MASTS AND BILLOWING SAILS TO TURN THE EARTH FROM DAY TO NIGHT AND BACK AGAIN. THANK YOU DOGS FOR BARKING AND HEARTS FOR BEATING. THANK YOU WINGS FOR FLAPPING AND COINS FOR FLIPPING. THANK YOU COURAGE AND WISDOM FOR SHOWING US HOW TO LET GO OF SEPARATE TRUTHS THAT WE HOLD IN SEPARATE HEARTS THAT KEEP US APART...SO WE CAN FIND THOSE TRUTHS AGAIN...ONLY THIS TIME TOGETHER...IN ONE HEART. THANK YOU GOD FOR HAVING SO MANY WONDERFUL IDEAS. GENTLE SPIRIT OF CREATION...YOU ARE THE BREAD AND BREATH OF OUR LIVES. AS WE CONSUME YOU, SO LET US BE CONSUMED BY OUR LOVE FOR YOU.

TABLE OF CONTENTS   vii

The spontaneous moment of *creation,* like the silence, is continuous throughout eternity.

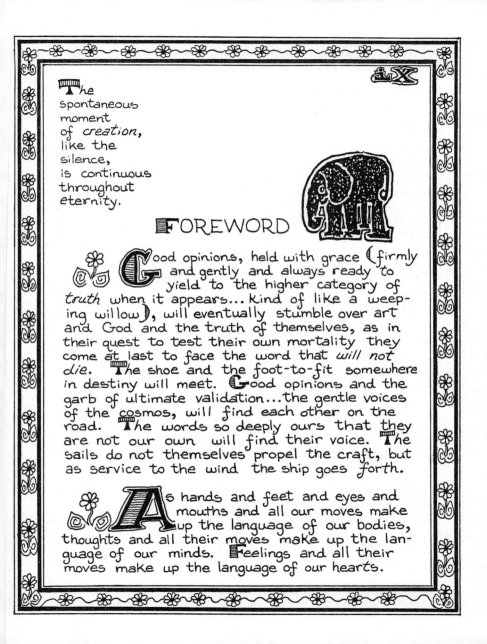

FOREWORD

Good opinions, held with grace (firmly and gently and always ready to yield to the higher category of *truth* when it appears... kind of like a weeping willow), will eventually stumble over art and God and the truth of themselves, as in their quest to test their own mortality they come at last to face the word that *will not die.* The shoe and the foot-to-fit somewhere in destiny will meet. Good opinions and the garb of ultimate validation...the gentle voices of the cosmos, will find each other on the road. The words so deeply ours that they are not our own will find their voice. The sails do not themselves propel the craft, but as service to the wind the ship goes *forth.*

As hands and feet and eyes and mouths and all our moves make up the language of our bodies, thoughts and all their moves make up the language of our minds. Feelings and all their moves make up the language of our hearts.

All our moves are language. All of them are language, and language is a medium of art. And art is a woman to woo and win. But beware. She is a woman who has no mercy. For the losers, even the dregs are too good. To the victors, she gives out consciousness like soup.

Art and consciousness try each other on for size. On and on and on again, they try each other out... on and on and on again until a fit is found... some kind of fit. In the give and take, both of them take form. They are both refined, reformed, increased; both of them are charged like batteries. The subtleties of intimate exchange illuminate and animate the process at the roots. Art is only intimacy searching for itself.

Devotion to an art or craft leads eventually to some perfection in its form. From there, the art or craft can give perfection back to us. In formulating thoughts and words and feelings into art, a blossoming occurs whereby we are made over and over and over again until finally we are tuned and playing in harmony with *The Orchestra of Being*, a melody to stir... a symphony to cultivate the soil of Creation. With every new development, it seems *before* was just a skeleton and *now* is living flesh. Art, like love and God and truth, it seems is always, for the first time, being only just uncovered. To so love art as in all things, her quiet, healing face to see... to so confuse, to so bemuse, her quiet, healing face is thee.

A bite away from truth, a writer's fishing line, it seems, is always cast. A writer's camera, always poised, a click away from truth, is waiting for a face that can't be seen with eyes but only words... is waiting for a scene that even dances past the glowing aura of the sunset blossom.

As you were leaving I mentioned something to you about resistance to truth being like a chinning bar.

"Resistance to truth is truth itself demanding strength of itself," I said. "Resistance to truth is truth in disguise." You were preparing to go out the door when you looked up at me.

"Precisely," you said. It was a sideward glance. You won't remember. I thought I noticed a glimmer of wonder in your eyes.

❀   ❀   ❀   ❀

Evolution endorses some requests for journeys into new forms of consciousness by granting a body or physical form or vehicle for taking the journey. For example, the chicken body was granted to endorse the journey into chicken consciousness. The watermelon body was granted to endorse the journey into water-melon consciousness. The human body was granted to endorse the journey into human consciousness. Books were granted to endorse the journey into the consciousness of a word.

❀ ❀ ❀ ❀

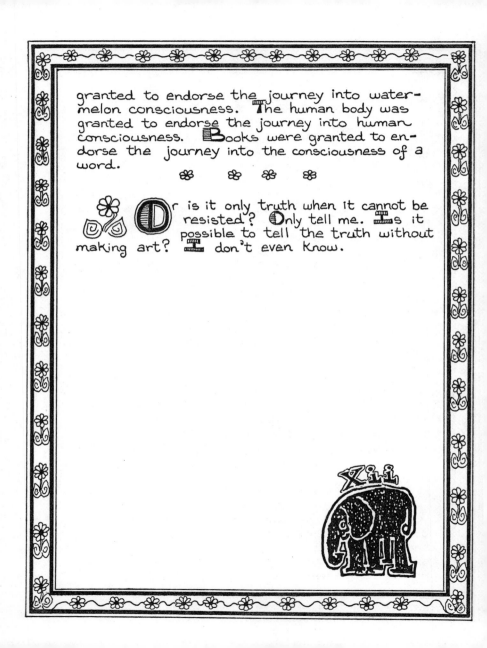

Or is it only truth when it cannot be resisted? Only tell me. Is it possible to tell the truth without making art? I don't even know.

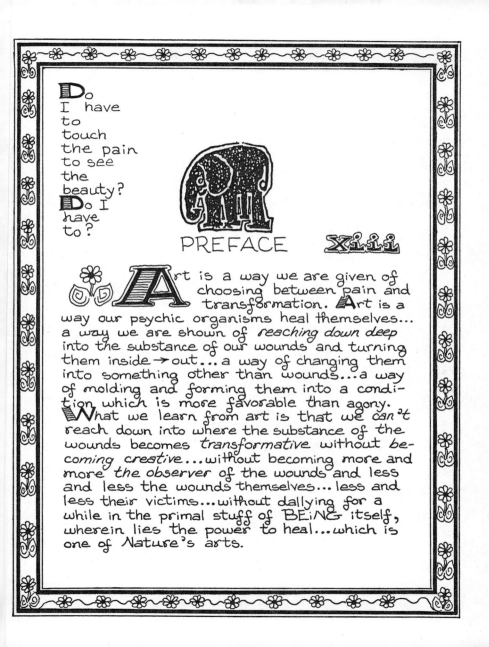

Do
I have
to
touch
the pain
to see
the
beauty?
Do I
have
to?

PREFACE

Art is a way we are given of choosing between pain and transformation. **A**rt is a way our psychic organisms heal themselves... a way we are shown of *reaching down deep* into the substance of our wounds and turning them inside → out... a way of changing them into something other than wounds... a way of molding and forming them into a condition which is more favorable than agony. **W**hat we learn from art is that we can't reach down into where the substance of the wounds becomes *transformative* without *becoming creative*... without becoming more and more *the observer* of the wounds and less and less the wounds themselves... less and less their victims... without dallying for a while in the primal stuff of BEING itself, wherein lies the power to heal... which is one of Nature's arts.

Another thing we learn from art is that pain brings us to a curious threshold in ourselves—and it is only a relatively *minor* shift in perspective...a movement of only a very small degree that carries us free of pain's hold on us and enters us into a whole new country where art is the power...not pain. This new country defies description, except that *with the entry*, we are suddenly <u>accelerated</u> in a way that brings every fragmentation together into something whole and every pathology out of the murk and cloud of *itself* to bathe in the light for a bit. Suddenly *the very moment of our life* feels like a launching pad for embarking on a great adventure. Perhaps the purpose of pain is to bring us to that threshold. (The purpose of art is certainly to carry us across it.) Perhaps surrendering to pain is turning tail and fleeing in the face of the enemy. (Making art is certainly digging in for a fight.) Perhaps it is wise to choose a way that teaches courage...as courage is rumored to have value.

To temper the unmerciful self-indulgence of artists with a redeeming virtue, there's another threshold that might be mentioned here at the advent of *Pillow Mountain*, for this threshold is the foundation for the book. There is a precious and precarious point on the creative roller coaster where the artist's struggle for life (through art) turns into the struggle for the life of the Earth... a point where our art becomes a clear outcry for help that penetrates far into the distant regions of the universe... and the universe responds with a bonafide rescue attempt. There's a point where the artist's struggle to fuse with the unrelenting creativity of *the moment* becomes the struggle of the Earth itself to secure the continuity of *Nature*, which is the prerequisite condition for life itself. This point is the threshold I'm talking about.

Civilization has become a threat to the continuity of nature on the Earth because its premise is rooted in fear. Civilization was conceived primarily as a refuge from fear (safety in numbers and safety behind walls ... anything to fend off the creeping willies). Civilization is a highly idealized, highly evolved protection scam... a primal response to fear... and as a response to fear, it *needs* fear to maintain its posture and keep its equilibrium....and fear needs enemies, conflicts, strife and war to maintain its posture and keep its equilibrium...for its own peace of mind... and so it manufactures them at its leisure. (Fear breeds contempt, making enemies, conflicts, strife and war very easy to sell.) But there is a corrosive element in fear that degrades unto death the living spirit and the living environment.

We are immersed in the most profound planetary urgencies. **W**e have built a whole civilization on *an insufficient premise*. **W**e have learned to compensate for that insufficiency by filling in its blanks with partial truths and now we are watching the *impartial untruths* on the other sides of our cultural coins turning to poison, wearing thin the fabric of our illusions, desecrating the natural world around us, stealing the breath from the Earth and corroding the rights of the future into dust. **A**s the poisons penetrate more and more deeply into the living systems of the Earth, our questions must deepen and our search for answers must intensify. **O**ne way or another *we will learn* that the ecology of *human thought and consciousness* and *the economy of Nature* are the right and left hands of one survival and one destiny.

To call our attention to *that in ourselves* which has cut us off from the natural world and to call us back to the Earth, we are visited by urgencies. **T**o deepen our inquiry into the source of an insufficiency and heighten our commitment to exposing the truth of it, we are visited by urgencies. **T**he work of this book is to translate urgency into art...to make it gentle without modifying or in any way disturbing the passion, which is the integrity of the urgency itself.

Reading into urgency a personal invitation to probe into the core of *Being* and dabble in the witchery of origin and cause is the liberty I take. From the license and the inspiration I find in that liberty, my art is born. In urgency, then, I find my invitation into the wellspring of creation. In art, I find urgency's kindest face...and if we don't accept her kindest face by invitation, we inherit her cruelest face by default. That's the law.

We are entering a new age and I believe art is the door...because when we enter into The Creative Act, we are facing off against fear and denying it the subjugation it has learned to expect from us...and this is precisely what is required. Making art is, in fact, refusing fear and subjugation their expected portions...and this refusing is the beginning of personal growth and planetary transformation.

Art is the door into the soul and the soul *is the material of transformation*...the stuff of life...the soup of it (where life is a soup)...*substance creative in itself*. Then order a bowl of it. Jump in the pot of it. Spice up the lot of it. It comes with the meal. Collaborating with *The Uncreated*, mingling with the mystical elements of *Being*, taking the impossible passions implicit in the human condition and changing them into things of beauty is the *work* of art...is the untrammeling of the human spirit that only art and falling in love allow. In all human enterprise, art alone courts the soul. Even the power of a religion lies in its stature as a work of art. Only art can make life work. Only love can make art live. Where loving is the artist, the soul is the canvas. Where living is the artist, the Earth is the canvas. In the ethics of art and the consciousness that they engender is the liberation of the spirit, the reclamation of the soul and the healing of this remarkable partnership called *Earth*.

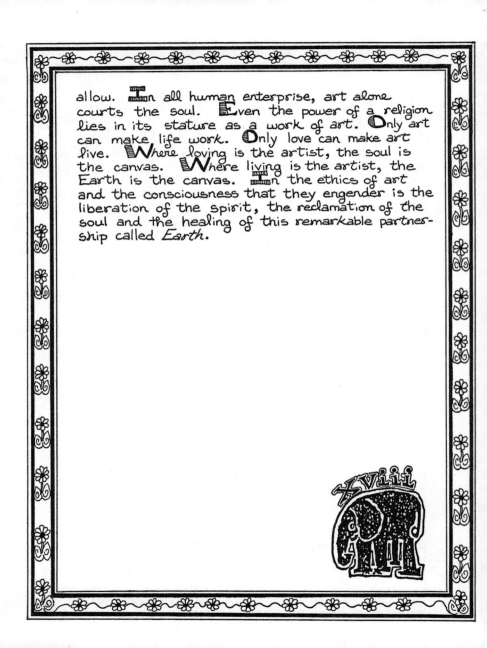

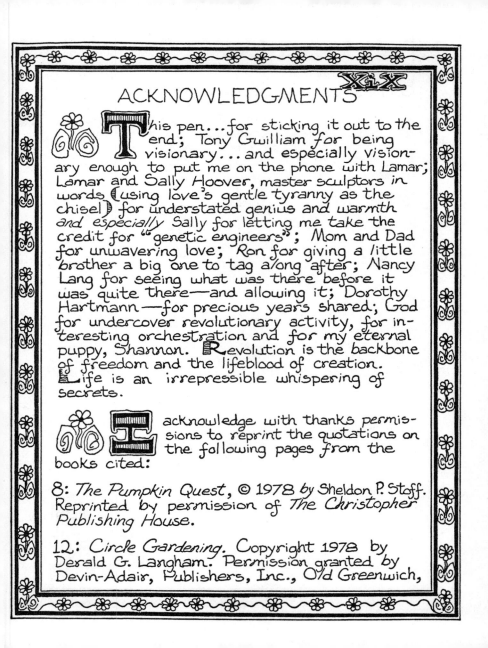

ACKNOWLEDGMENTS

This pen... for sticking it out to the end; Tony Gwilliam for being visionary... and especially visionary enough to put me on the phone with Lamar; Lamar and Sally Hoover, master sculptors in words (using love's gentle tyranny as the chisel) for understated genius and warmth and especially Sally for letting me take the credit for "genetic engineers"; Mom and Dad for unwavering love; Ron for giving a little brother a big one to tag along after; Nancy Lang for seeing what was there before it was quite there—and allowing it; Dorothy Hartmann—for precious years shared; God for undercover revolutionary activity, for interesting orchestration and for my eternal puppy, Shannon. **R**evolution is the backbone of freedom and the lifeblood of creation. **L**ife is an irrepressible whispering of secrets.

I acknowledge with thanks permissions to reprint the quotations on the following pages from the books cited:

8: *The Pumpkin Quest*, © 1978 by Sheldon P. Stoff. Reprinted by permission of *The Christopher Publishing House.*

12: *Circle Gardening.* Copyright 1978 by Derald G. Langham. Permission granted by Devin-Adair, Publishers, Inc., Old Greenwich,

Connecticut 06870. All rights reserved.

61: Neumann, Erich; *The Origins and History of Consciousness*, translated by R.F. Hull. Copyright 1954 by the Bollingen Foundation. Reprinted by permission of Princeton University Press.

167-68: *Black Elk Speaks: Being the life story of a holy man of the Oglala Sioux*, as told through John G. Neihardt (Flaming Rainbow). Copyright 1932 by John G. Neihardt; Copyright © 1961 by the John G. Neihardt Trust. Reprinted by permission of the University of Nebraska Press.

The quotation on page 51 is from William Penn's *Some Fruits of Solitude*, first published in 1693. On page 77, Aristotle is quoted from Benjamin Jowett's classic translation of *Politics*, first published in 1885.

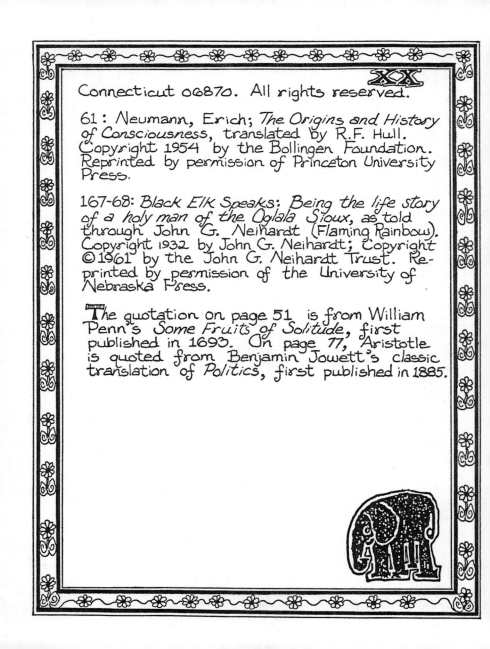

INTRODUCTiON

Life is an ocean. Love is a ship.

When I first noticed the cloud formation
billowing
up
like a volcano
out of a rolling, white blanket of cotton puffs
that stretched unbroken across the sky in every
direction, I didn't know that it was
Pillow
Mountain. But then the plane *turned*
on its right wing
and headed in its direction.
Suddenly I was a
snowman
sent soaring
by some outrageous *destiny* to *splash* into a monu-
mental TOWER of white fluff. Then the name
Pillow Mountain was spoken from someplace deep
inside of me and I knew that
that was what it was...and I was the only one on
the plane who knew. I wanted to get up and
yell out to all the other passengers to LOOK OUT
THE WiNDOW because nobody had ever seen
Pillow Mountain before and no one would ever
see it
again
...but I didn't think
anyone
would understand
so I kept
quiet.

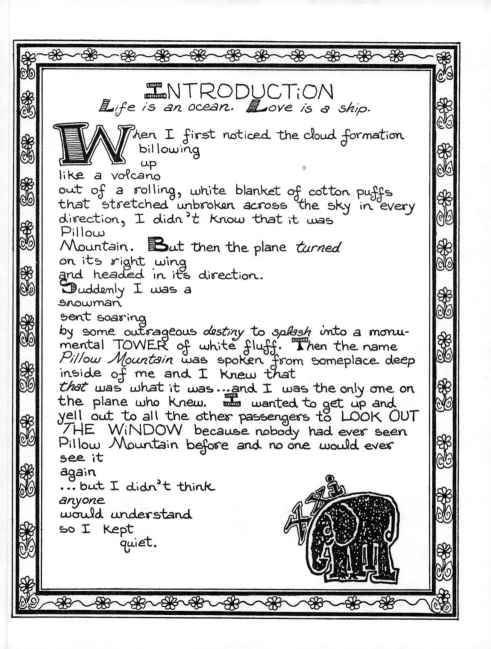

WHEN WINGS ARE ONLY
LENT TO BIRDS, WHEN ANGELS
DANCE BETWEEN THE WORDS,
WHEN ONLY SECRETS THEN ARE
HEARD....WHEN SECRETS THEN
ARE HEARD.

To secure the positive, creative
evolution of life on the planet,
catch hold of the silence that falls
so gently after the laughter, after
the tears. Plant the endless moment
in a field of soft grass. Listen
for tomorrow.

LONG SPOONS   1

These crazy buses! They go
screaming down the road like
angry dragons. Back and forth
from Pondicherry to Madras, they beep their
horns... their screeching horns, the whole way
like nothing is important. They're packed so
full of dark-skinned people that their eyes
reach out to you...eyes so deep they give themselves to you. They pass so close your cells
are changed.

The road to Pondicherry is narrow,
paved with asphalt and lined with
huts and shops of hardened mud
or bricks with roofs of woven palm-leaf mats
called "keet," overlaid with straw, that only last
three years before they start to leak. Thatched,
they last for eight.

Everyone is on the narrow road, it
seems...mobs of bare and dark-
skinned feet; herds of goats;
shining black oxen bulging at the middles, their
horns scooping and swirling backward about as
far as their long snouts poke forward (as

if for balancing their heads); white bullocks and cows with humps on their backs and horns (usually painted...usually one a different color from the other), pulling ox carts brimming over with a palm-leaf harvest; pedal-powered rickshaws manned by courageous, lonely drivers lumbering along with entire families of six or seven stuffed in behind; small, white dogs collapsed from the heat, barely panting, lying on the side of the road; chickens; roosters; giant black beetles with bright red or yellow spots on their backs, gleaming like porcelain figures on display in a gift shop window...and then the endless flow of tiny, gray or ebony taxicabs and cars, motorbikes and scooters, all tooting their funny horns; ordinary cyclists like me, often riding with two and even three aboard, all clinging their little bells...and those crazy buses ...all going here and there.

They pay priests to perform *pujas* over each bus so they don't kill anyone or get into accidents. A puja is a spiritual registration service for motor vehicles (and other things) where men in trousers and Miami Beach tourist shirts and golden women wrapped in silken saris place guavas, melons and tomatoes under all the wheels, scatter flowers generously around and carry burning incense through the four-wheeled dragons, chanting all the while. Then when you come by a couple of hours later, the bus is gone, everything has been convincingly crushed and some bus driver is on his way from Pondicherry to Madras and back again, beeping his horn the whole way with nothing coming to harm. Nicklaus, my friend from Auroville, explained to me what they were doing when we bicycled past one of the ceremonies still in progress next to *The Governor's Palace* in Pondy.

※

"Go to India," Navroop had said to me when I met her at a poetry reading at *The Blacksmith House* on Brattle Street in Harvard Square. Just six months had passed since Molly had left me for Alan Gimble. Joshie was ten. He stayed with me until I was strong enough to make it on my own. Or strong enough to give him up. Not quite the same.

Since standing on the back porch with John and Amy and watching my trusty Ford van burn in some early morning darkness, five months had passed. Shadows dancing with the flickering lights against the houses and the trees. My four-wheeled friend was leaving me too.

"This must be my time for losing things," I said to John. Amy was bundled in a blanket. Her fragile face mirrored merciless bursts of flames. Her eyes were alight. She was Helen watching Troy burn from a turret in the center of the golden city. I was wondering if my time for getting things would ever come again.

"The life here dumps you inside yourself," Nicklaus says to me, riding two aboard my rented bicycle on our way into Pondicherry to buy a glass of orange juice for his birthday.

"Even if you don't want to go inside, you have to," he says.

We ride through a dusty Tamil village along a bumpy road, weaving in and out among the huts, past women gathered at the well, past the village school where fifty children are packed in like sardines beneath a grass roof suspended precariously on top of some rickety poles. Fifty shining faces turn our way.

Past a funeral procession we ride. The lifeless body of a meagre, ancient man rests underneath a blanket of garlands and flowers on a wooden pallet lifted high above the heads of somber bearers. Pressed against the eager lips of a villager strutting in the lead of the procession, a silver trumpet sets the tone and marks the pace: "Bill Bailey Won't You Please Come Home." ♫ ♩ ❀ ✿ ♩ ♪ ♩. The notes come prancing out. Somehow it seems to work. It seems to fit.

Nicklaus arrived in Auroville two years ago from Germany. He isn't short or tall; his hair is dark and close cropped, his face is full and deep and strong and almost sharp except the softness of his spirit rounds him off. From the beginning of his stay here he has worked on *The Matrimandir*, a great concrete sphere nearly ten stories high that stands in the center of the area designated for the international township of fifty thousand people that they speak of building. They've been building the sphere for over ten years now and it's about two-thirds of the way completed.

Matrimandir means "soul of the Mother," the idea being that the first thing you make is the soul and then everything else takes form around it according to spiritual principle and natural law. It houses one great room for meditation. Nicklaus lives in the worker's camp, adjacent to the worksite. They have sit-down toilets there.

It is a striking thing to see a great bald sphere of concrete-white towering over trees still fresh from the season of their planting. The whole eight square kilometers, surely given gladly by the government of India for this aggressive, starry vision, was parched and desolate just ten short years ago and now a million trees are down, cooling off the air, softening the land and calling back the spirit that often flees the wake of humankind.

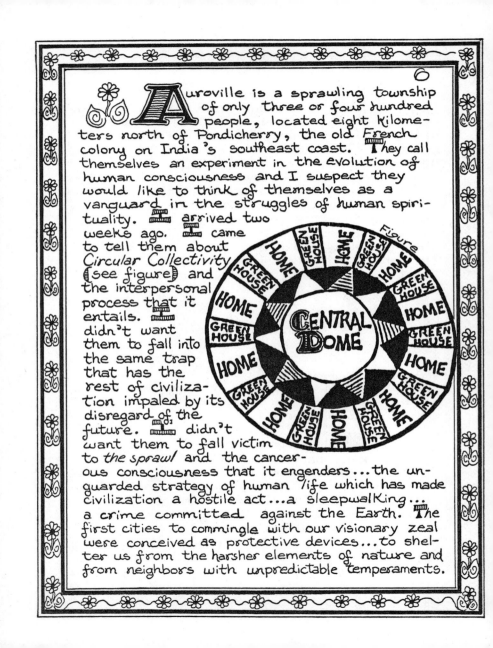

Auroville is a sprawling township of only three or four hundred people, located eight kilometers north of Pondicherry, the old *French* colony on India's southeast coast. They call themselves an experiment in the evolution of human consciousness and I suspect they would like to think of themselves as a vanguard in the struggles of human spirituality. ▦ arrived two weeks ago. ▦ came to tell them about *Circular Collectivity* (see figure) and the interpersonal process that it entails. ▦ didn't want them to fall into the same trap that has the rest of civilization impaled by its disregard of the future. ▦ didn't want them to fall victim to *the sprawl* and the cancerous consciousness that it engenders...the unguarded strategy of human *life* which has made civilization a hostile act...a sleepwalking... a crime committed against the Earth. The first cities to commingle with our visionary zeal were conceived as protective devices...to shelter us from the harsher elements of nature and from neighbors with unpredictable temperaments.

Figure

HOME · GREEN HOUSE · HOME · GREEN HOUSE · HOME · GREEN HOUSE · HOME · GREEN HOUSE · HOME · GREEN HOUSE · HOME · GREEN HOUSE · HOME · GREEN HOUSE · HOME · GREEN HOUSE

CENTRAL DOME

The new cities have to be conceived to address that same unpredictability as a sacred ingredient in our spirits...and to protect nature from us. The secret is living in harmony with the wilderness...learning how to balance the concentration and dispersion of human population with the needs of the wilderness... and the circle is the teacher. The circle is the balance. The circle is the integrity of the wilderness and the integrity of the wilderness is the power and the breath of the Earth. The wilderness is the firstborn of the Earth. Civilization is the second. Until the two siblings of the Earth are at peace with each other, how can there be peace in ourselves? The ground here is red clay. Aurovillians all have red feet.

Eastward, through a staggered army of bending palms cropped all the way up to barely leafing tops, I watch the Bay of Bengal grabbing at the fine, white sand of the Coromandel Coast. On the narrow road to Pondicherry, my bicycle leans against a stone guard wall on a little bridge that spans the empty bed of a rivulet where water, in the rainy season, races to the sea. Children gather around without a sound to watch me scrawling in my notebook. It's open season on wondering and watching. Their glance is an embrace...like a covering of mist.

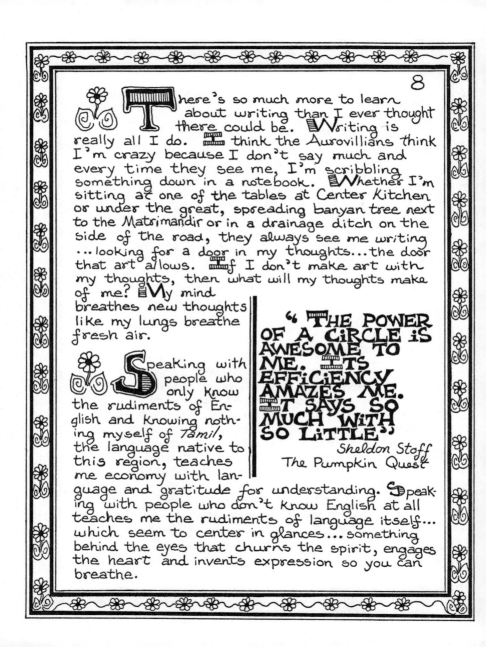

There's so much more to learn about writing than I ever thought there could be. Writing is really all I do. I think the Aurovillians think I'm crazy because I don't say much and every time they see me, I'm scribbling something down in a notebook. Whether I'm sitting at one of the tables at Center Kitchen or under the great, spreading banyan tree next to the Matrimandir or in a drainage ditch on the side of the road, they always see me writing ...looking for a door in my thoughts...the door that art allows. If I don't make art with my thoughts, then what will my thoughts make of me? My mind breathes new thoughts like my lungs breathe fresh air.

Speaking with people who only know the rudiments of English and knowing nothing myself of *Tamil*, the language native to this region, teaches me economy with language and gratitude for understanding. Speaking with people who don't know English at all teaches me the rudiments of language itself... which seem to center in glances... something behind the eyes that churns the spirit, engages the heart and invents expression so you can breathe.

> " THE POWER OF A CIRCLE IS AWESOME TO ME. ITS EFFICIENCY AMAZES ME. IT SAYS SO MUCH WITH SO LITTLE"
>
> *Sheldon Stoff*
> *The Pumpkin Quest*

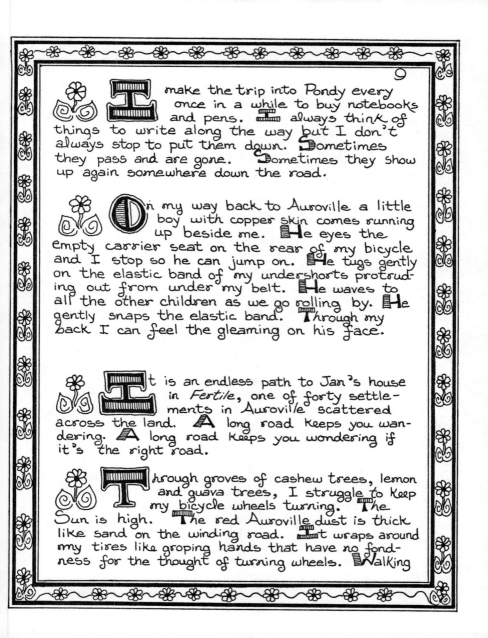

I make the trip into Pondy every once in a while to buy notebooks and pens. I always think of things to write along the way but I don't always stop to put them down. Sometimes they pass and are gone. Sometimes they show up again somewhere down the road.

On my way back to Auroville a little boy with copper skin comes running up beside me. He eyes the empty carrier seat on the rear of my bicycle and I stop so he can jump on. He tugs gently on the elastic band of my undershorts protruding out from under my belt. He waves to all the other children as we go rolling by. He gently snaps the elastic band. Through my back I can feel the gleaming on his face.

It is an endless path to Jan's house in *Fertile*, one of forty settlements in Auroville scattered across the land. A long road keeps you wandering. A long road keeps you wondering if it's the right road.

Through groves of cashew trees, lemon and guava trees, I struggle to keep my bicycle wheels turning. The Sun is high. The red Auroville dust is thick like sand on the winding road. It wraps around my tires like groping hands that have no fondness for the thought of turning wheels. Walking would be easier but I've lost enough already to the path. But seems I won't give up my seat without a fight.

The road turns sharply to the right and suddenly the trees are taller and fuller. The air is fresher. The leaves are thicker and greener like the woods back home when I was a little boy in Baltimore and everything was vine-covered forts and hiding from each other in the woodland thickets and bushes at the end of the block. The road firms and the wheels of my bicycle roll easily along.

Two Tamil villagers are helping Johnny put a ferroconcrete roof on his house because his thatched roof started leaking in the middle of the rainy season last year. The cost of palm leaves for roofing has more than tripled in the last two years. In the long run, the cement roof will be a good investment. Ferroconcrete is versatile. You can work it into any form you want. And the villagers work for very little money.

Jan's house is next to Johnny's. Hers is a funny double decker box... a little tower with one small room to a floor and a brick pond in front, laid in a circle about twelve yards across, like a big mosaic soup bowl planted in the ground. Together, they look like a handle and a hoop. The house stands right on the rim of the pond and seems to lean a bit over the water like it's thinking about falling in.

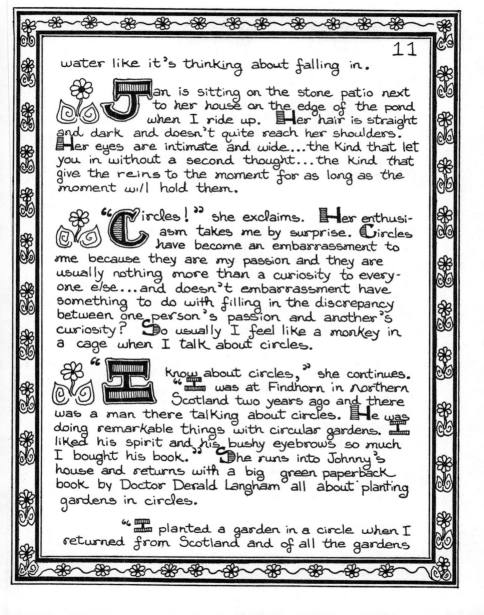

Jan is sitting on the stone patio next to her house on the edge of the pond when I ride up. Her hair is straight and dark and doesn't quite reach her shoulders. Her eyes are intimate and wide...the kind that let you in without a second thought...the kind that give the reins to the moment for as long as the moment will hold them.

"**C**ircles!" she exclaims. Her enthusiasm takes me by surprise. Circles have become an embarrassment to me because they are my passion and they are usually nothing more than a curiosity to everyone else...and doesn't embarrassment have something to do with filling in the discrepancy between one person's passion and another's curiosity? So usually I feel like a monkey in a cage when I talk about circles.

"**I** know about circles," she continues. "I was at Findhorn in northern Scotland two years ago and there was a man there talking about circles. He was doing remarkable things with circular gardens. I liked his spirit and his bushy eyebrows so much I bought his book." She runs into Johnny's house and returns with a big green paperback book by Doctor Derald Langham all about planting gardens in circles.

"**I** planted a garden in a circle when I returned from Scotland and of all the gardens

I've ever planted, that's the only one to regenerate itself the following year," she says.

As I finger the pages like a sacred text, she talks about the circle of the pond in front of her house. She says people from all over Auroville comment about her house being the most peaceful place in the township and she's certain it has to do with the circle of the pond in front of her house. I watch a lizard skitter barely free of a frog's sudden strike on the brick-lined rim of the pond, thick with algae green. I think about a square pond and other shaped ponds and the feeling of peace is gone.

"**P**eace has something to do with a circle and the way things speak and balance on its edge," I say. Jan is packing to leave for Australia in two days. Your best allies are always leaving for Australia in two days. I think the lizard was too big for froggie anyway.

"**O**ne of the interesting aspects of circle gardening is that of watching the seedlings... start to grow at a more or less steady rate until suddenly something happens and they take on a new life," Doctor Langham writes. "From that time on they have a new glow and an expression of vigor, & health, and well-being that continues throughout the remainder of their life cycle."

A picture of Doctor Langham with a lawn mower catches my eye. His eyebrows, in good Scottish tradition, are giant, fluffy-white caterpillars standing guard over everything he sees and teaching him the magic of the Earth. He's standing in the middle of a whole constellation of circular gardens showing how easy it is to mow the grassy spaces between them all. I'm picturing a bunch of people happily planted in a circle.

Not only does the vitality of plants increase in circular gardens but yield also increases. Dr. Langham seems to think this is because being in a circle links each individual plant more directly with the elemental forces of nature. This is already a primary postulate of my life. A circle, after all, defines a center and gives it life. Would a center not then reciprocate by giving increasing life and definition back out again to members of the circle? My guess is that the game proceeds as back and forth as back and forth can be until the circle is itself a living thing.

If a circle is a living thing, a circle of living things becomes a double living thing. Circulating life times two, regenerating life times two, a circle is a way of multiplying. Circulating life times two, regenerating life times two, who's to say, once started, that the multiplying stops with two? Once started, who's to say it stops at all. Falling in love works on the same principle.

There is a mystical circle whose members searching for each other are life searching for itself. Ashu Jain is a poet and a student of chemical engineering at a university east of Delhi and far to the north of Pondicherry and Madras. He was one of a group of twenty Indian students who had won a week in Auroville, sponsored by the Indian government, by writing essays on peace. He saw me writing and came over to see what I was writing about.

He told me my idea of living in circles reminded him of a story in ancient Hindu literature about the difference between heaven and hell. In both heaven and hell, according to the story, everyone has these long spoons.

"In hell," Ashu said, "everyone tries feeding themselves and it doesn't work because the spoons are so long." (Apparently everybody is requested to hold the spoons at their very ends so as not to poke anyone in the eye...making the spoon part of the spoon too far away from the mouth part of us to make it useful for getting anything *inside* of us.)

In heaven, needless to say, everyone feeds each other and it works wonderfully well. ❁ ❁ ❁ ❁

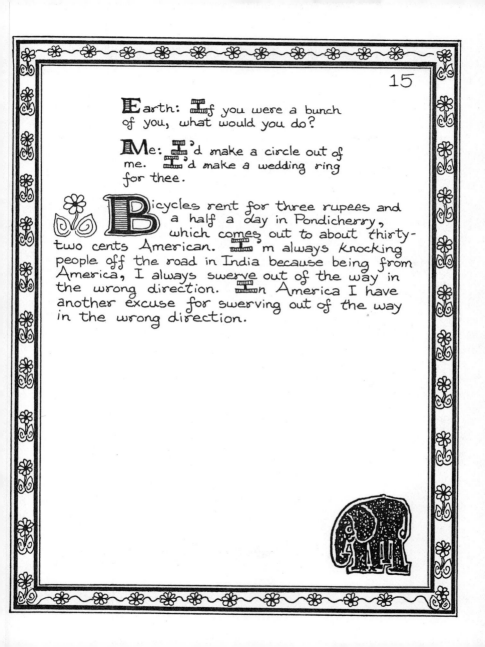

Earth: If you were a bunch of you, what would you do?

Me: I'd make a circle out of me. I'd make a wedding ring for thee.

Bicycles rent for three rupees and a half a day in Pondicherry, which comes out to about thirty-two cents American. I'm always knocking people off the road in India because being from America, I always swerve out of the way in the wrong direction. In America I have another excuse for swerving out of the way in the wrong direction.

MAYONNAiSE

Once when I was living in a commune on Massachusetts Avenue in north Cambridge, I walked past the friendly neighborhood grocery store a few doors down from the house, glanced in the big plate glass window bordering the sidewalk and saw this man pinching the cashier woman's nose. She was all red and flustered and trying to get away but the man wouldn't let her so I walked in like the White Knight, asked the man what he was doing, told him he shouldn't and suggested that he try being ashamed of himself for treating someone like that.

This seemed to get the man very upset because he turned to this other man he was with, asked him with an unmistakable air of disbelief if he'd heard what I said, started rabbling and babbling about how much nerve I had and who the hell did I think I was, but he didn't pinch her nose anymore. I bought a small jar of Miracle Whip for forty-five cents and the cashier woman came over and offered to help me find what I was looking for and she looked up at me like I was Jesus Christ and I said no thank you, that I just wanted a jar of mayonnaise.

Daniel Small

Names were invented so everyone doesn't try opening all the mail all at once.

GREAT BOOKS 19

After it's been read, a book rests differently, more nobly on the shelf. A heart rides differently, more freely in its casing after it's been touched. The first time I looked out the window of my second-floor dormitory room at St. John's College in Annapolis, Maryland, I saw Tom Crosby. He was out on the field behind the dormitory all by himself kicking a football around. Looking past him I could see to the tennis courts and scarcely scattered trees that dotted the back campus, then on all the way down to the Severn River, just above where it empties into the Chesapeake Bay (where later on that term, in the spring, Tom and I would hold up Navy maneuvers for twenty minutes while we paddled past in our canoe... the Naval Academy is the next door down). The first time I saw him, it wasn't quite fall. Anticipations were astir. A great adventure was at hand. The semester was just beginning.

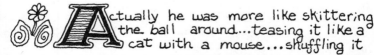

Actually he was more like skittering the ball around...teasing it like a cat with a mouse...shuffling it through the grass with unusual abandon and playfulness that wouldn't let anything stand in its way. He was a glimpse of something deep inside of me that I would have to find one day. There was a golden handle to a missing part of me. I decided I would find the handle. When something deep inside of me exploded out onto the field to join him, the decision had already been made.

I didn't know they called St. John's *The Great Books School*. When a little red Yamaha *Twin One Hundred* motorcycle with dual carburetors, dual exhausts and me on board went modestly whizzing past a highway sign announcing a distance of twenty miles to Washington and eighteen to Annapolis, I didn't know they called St. John's St. John's. I only knew there was a college in Annapolis, that I needed to find a school and Annapolis felt warmer and two miles closer than Washington.

St. John's has been accused of being so conservative that it's radical. While you're reading the ancient Greeks, you're also learning their language. You're constructing the geometry with Euclid, the heavens with Ptolemy, you're fighting their wars, contending with their philosophers, following the trail of their drama and grabbing at the tail of their comedy. The curriculum is a guided tour into our cultural origins hosted by *the classics*, finding its itinerary and its asides in the patterns set by *the tradition of inquiry and resolution* as it has actually cleared its path for itself through the underbrush of human emergence ...leaving markers, staking claims wherever destiny saw fit to allow.

The seminar is the stage for the drama of the college to unfold. Answering the chiming of the bell that shocks the quiet air to life just after darkness falls...the ruthless call to seminar...you cross the short brick plaza to McDowell Hall. You climb its hallowed flights of stairs and enter one of many hallowed rooms, finely paneled, profoundly haunted by the quaking ghosts of overunderstood authors, the tormented spirits of unresolved arguments and unspoken thoughts left for the vultures to pick at the bones...all lingering, ever pulsing in the woodwork. You take your place in the lull before the storm, around a great square oaken table. Two tutors are poised like referees at opposing ends and twelve or fourteen tutees are gathered around, all ready to follow Plato out of the shadowy cave of images and into the light of pure forms...all ready to hop on a renegade raft with Albert Einstein and Huckleberry Finn and drop trembling lines into the muddy Mississippi to see what dares to take the hooks. It's all too magical to become routine. Quickening spirits present by provoking spirits past is dangerous and adventuresome business.

"The books are the bones for the puppies to sharpen their teeth," Mr. Scofield said to me outside of the coffee shop in the basement of McDowell.

"A teacher of mine told me that when I was a student here," he said. And now he'd passed it on to me.

In seminar, Mr. Scofield rarely said a word. But you could feel him there, guiding and protecting little bites and nibbles, fragile puppy teeth, helping them come in straight and true and ultimately suited to the job. He rarely spoke. But that's not true. And now he's gone. That also isn't true.

Doesn't wisdom move in circles? Doesn't knowledge form in circles? Around the oaken table, I'm pretty certain that a circle here is forming. All cuddled in our learning beds beneath our woolen learning blankets, our dimming flashlights following the lines that some heroic writer snatched out of a dragon's mouth—wedged between the teeth, with just a pen to prod them free, with just a pen to save himself—I'm pretty sure a circle here is forming. Following the lines that countless other eyes have followed and countless more will claim...stumbling over insights that no one else would think to look for, no one else would dare to find...taking our inheritance in stride, just piece by piece,

I'm certain that a circle here is forming. It is made of characters and thoughts and stories ...wondrous stories. One by one, each takes its place around a circle forming, each a golden piece.

The ghosts of famous authors live here. St. John's makes a home for wayward ghosts, you see. An interesting charity.

Einstein's face by *Joyce Gerrish*

24

FEET, BEING PUT AT THE BOTTOM OF US, MAKE A USEFUL CONTACT WITH THE GROUND, AS FAR AS GETTING FROM HERE TO THERE IS CONCERNED. HUMILITY, BEING PUT AT THE BOTTOM OF US IN A DIFFERENT WAY, ALSO MAKES A USEFUL CONTACT, BUT WITH A DIFFERENT KIND OF GROUND——AS FAR AS GETTING FROM HERE TO THERE IS CONCERNED.

ONE MOMENT

To take our watches by surprise,
one moment
lives
beyond the thought of time.
Past the limits of eternity,
from one end to another,
one tiny moment spreads its wings.
A wing span spreading way beyond the
future and the past, so much pours through
the tiny portal of a moment, like the pupil
of
an
eye...
so small
to count a multitude of
stars.
To enter through a tiny door
a sea of endless possibility
is the genius of the universe.
To venture ever farther in a room that's
getting
    smaller...
to fit the billowing scope of endless being
in the binding vessel of a shrinking moment,
if it's not the object of the game,
is probably
a strategy
for
winning.

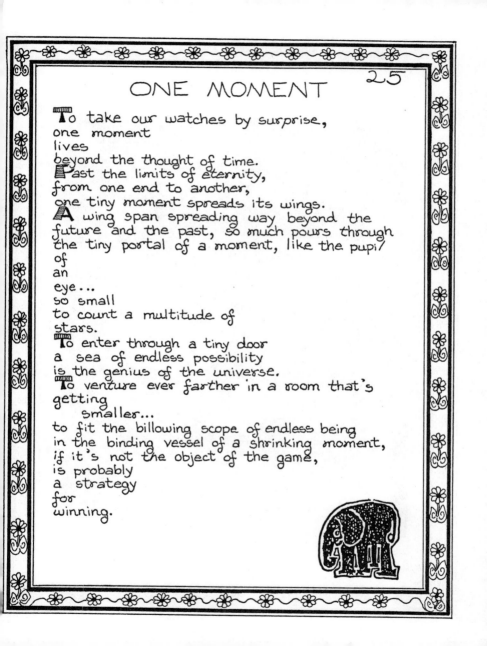

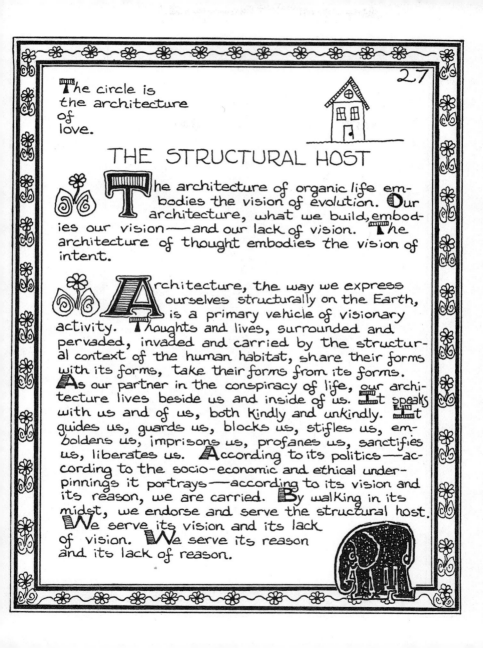

The circle is
the architecture
of
love.

THE STRUCTURAL HOST

The architecture of organic life embodies the vision of evolution. Our architecture, what we build, embodies our vision——and our lack of vision. The architecture of thought embodies the vision of intent.

Architecture, the way we express ourselves structurally on the Earth, is a primary vehicle of visionary activity. Thoughts and lives, surrounded and pervaded, invaded and carried by the structural context of the human habitat, share their forms with its forms, take their forms from its forms. As our partner in the conspiracy of life, our architecture lives beside us and inside of us. It speaks with us and of us, both kindly and unkindly. It guides us, guards us, blocks us, stifles us, emboldens us, imprisons us, profanes us, sanctifies us, liberates us. According to its politics——according to the socio-economic and ethical underpinnings it portrays——according to its vision and its reason, we are carried. By walking in its midst, we endorse and serve the structural host. We serve its vision and its lack of vision. We serve its reason and its lack of reason.

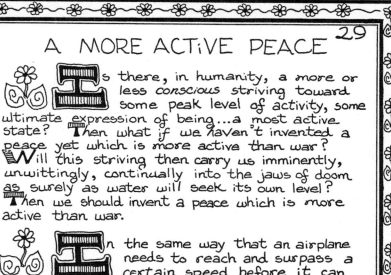

A MORE ACTiVE PEACE

Is there, in humanity, a more or less *conscious* striving toward some peak level of activity, some ultimate expression of being...a most active state? Then what if we haven't invented a peace yet which is more active than war? Will this striving then carry us imminently, unwittingly, continually into the jaws of doom as surely as water will seek its own level? Then we should invent a peace which is more active than war.

In the same way that an airplane needs to reach and surpass a certain speed before it can become airborne, perhaps there is a certain level of *creative intensity* or activity that has to be ventured and surpassed before our wings pop out...before we get to *lift off* of our metaphorical feet, break free of the metaphorical ground, leave behind us the metaphorical ground rules and enter fully into the realm governed by the aerodynamics of wonder and trust. Short of that certain level, everything is subject to a pathology of deficiency...and only in the realm of pathology does war dare to try passing itself off as a viable form of human expression. Perhaps peace is not the absence of conflicts but *the symphony of conflicts*, which having accelerated beyond that certain level of creative activity, has undergone the transformation to harmony and accord under the baton of wonder's architect.

To find the gift,
the moment of giving,
the way of unwrapping...
this is yoga...this is
art.

THE GiRAFFE

Sometimes I'll notice someone off in the distance, get a sense that it's some particular person and then watch it actually turn out to be that *very* person. **F**irst I'll say to myself that there was no way I could have discerned even a single feature of the distant figure, let alone successfully identified the entire person...that it must have just been a good guess or a coincidence. **B**ut then I'll wonder if there might be a sense of who a person is that gets transmitted even before you have a chance to see who it is...as though who you're going to see is already a memory inside you...as though whatever you're becoming already knows what it is and is sending out messages even before it's come to be...like a dream already knowing whether or not it's going to come true.

After talking to somebody once in Harvard Square in Cambridge in front of what was then *Hungry Charlie's* about whether or not you could put a saddle on a giraffe (whether their necks sloped directly down to their rumps or if they went down more perpendicularly and then *over*, leaving their backs more horizontal and more suitable for saddles...it had to do with a solution to the Middle East crisis that I was considering), I wandered across the street, past the subway station, past *The Harvard Coop* and rounded *Nini's Corner* where, happening coincidentally to glance up at the magazines displayed a little bit above eye-level on the outside racks, I noticed a magazine called *Miami Beach Life*. Prancing on the sand near the fringe of a green and laughing oasis, three Arabs, their eyes dark and piercing, their forms delicately framed with black veils and flowing black robes, two of them riding zebras, the third nobly mounted on a spotted giraffe, were peering out at me from the brightly colored painting on the cover.

It was like finding a letter addressed to me lying in a road I'd never trod before. It was like returning to the Earth after being away for ages and landing in the middle of a surprise party when no one even knew I was coming. New synapses sparked and ignited in my brain like skyrockets and flares, illuminating distant and remote regions of my consciousness. Time and again, laughter bubbled to the fragile surface of itself, time and again to get smothered in its last moment of containment by wonder's now regular pulse. I greeted the surge inside of me...the wave that wonder rides... the tide that brings it in.

Ecstatic, bewildered, I pulled a crinkled dollar bill from my pants pocket, paid the purchase price for one copy of *Miami Beach Life* and, clutching it to my breast, ran down to

Zum Zum's on the next corner to see if a friend of mine who was a waitress there was working that night.

She was there. Through ten-foot-high plate glass windows I watched Mary Ellen clearing dishes off the counter for the few late evening customers sitting around inside. I didn't go in. Owning a copy of *Miami Beach Life* seemed suddenly like a caging of something wild and free.

The newsstand attendant accepted the magazine back and returned my dollar with no questions asked. I stuffed the same crinkled bill back in my pocket and walked past *Nini's Corner* every chance I got after that. I learned how to pretend the magazine wasn't there at all so I could stroll by and catch it by surprise. Sometimes it would almost jump off the rack. Then one day, the green and laughing oasis, the giraffe, the two zebras and the three Arabs with the dark and piercing eyes were gone.

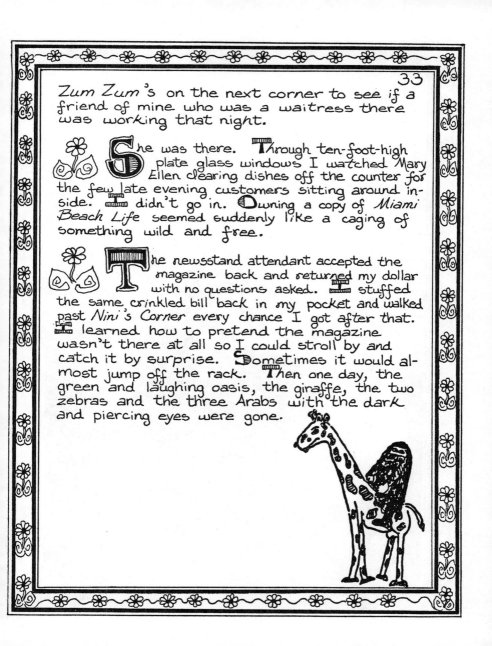

MiRACLES

The perception of a miracle is a critical part of the actual occurrence. A miracle is an organism...an actual living thing with its own personality, its own integrity and its own eyes. When we perceive a miracle, we become its eyes...magic crystal window-lakes through which it peers and sees itself. Looking outward at ourselves, suddenly all things in the outside world become parts of our own bodies...its organs, its flows, its junctures and rhythms. Suddenly, looking inward entails an outward perspective. Looking outward, we see our own insides dancing before our eyes.

WHAT TO DO WITH GENIUS... WHAT TO DO WITH GENIUS... ONLY ART KNOWS WHAT TO DO WITH GENIUS. GENIUS IS THE SPIRIT TO RIDE THE WAVE ETERNAL. ART WILL GIVE THE SPIRIT FORM AND GRACE AND DARING. LOVE WILL GIVE IT REASON.

36

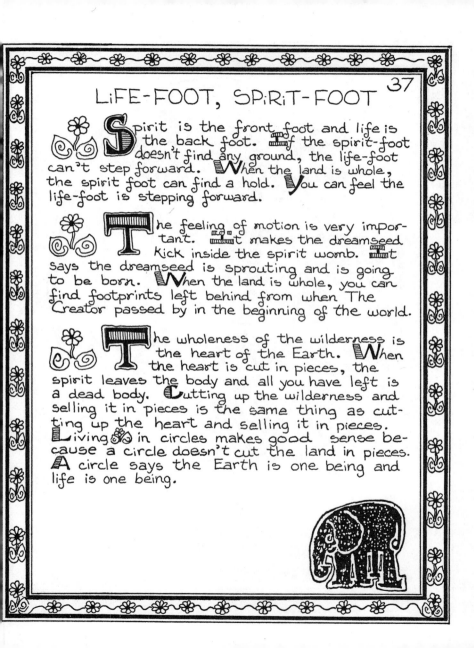

LiFE-FOOT, SPiRiT-FOOT

Spirit is the front foot and life is the back foot. If the spirit-foot doesn't find any ground, the life-foot can't step forward. **W**hen the land is whole, the spirit foot can find a hold. **Y**ou can feel the life-foot is stepping forward.

The feeling of motion is very important. It makes the dreamseed kick inside the spirit womb. It says the dreamseed is sprouting and is going to be born. **W**hen the land is whole, you can find footprints left behind from when The Creator passed by in the beginning of the world.

The wholeness of the wilderness is the heart of the Earth. **W**hen the heart is cut in pieces, the spirit leaves the body and all you have left is a dead body. **C**utting up the wilderness and selling it in pieces is the same thing as cutting up the heart and selling it in pieces. **L**iving in circles makes good sense because a circle doesn't cut the land in pieces. **A** circle says the Earth is one being and life is one being.

Thoughts and dreams, thought and unthought, dreamt and undreamt; inspirations received and refused, conceived and confused, acted and unacted upon, compose and conduct the symphony. We don't create. We merely portray more and less accurately the perfect wonder of what is already made by God.

A THOUSAND TiMES BEGUN

A thousand times begun, a thousand starts not true enough to carry through a noble race, a thousand jumps not high enough to catch the magic wind that gives lift to the merest fins and turns them into wings, a thousand swords not long enough, a thousand wounds not deep enough to reach the other side of pain, how long have I been writing? Searching for the blossom of my seed, how long have I been writing? Should I have known that writing, endless writing is my ears' attuning, endless tuning...tuning into voices past the planets, speaking closer than inside of me? Should I have known that reaching deep inside myself with words was reaching out beyond the stars?

To find a sparkling brook beneath the Earth whose source is well beyond the sky, there is a well to dig. How long have I been digging? When I find water, will I know I'm drinking from a well beyond the sky?

Drilling for the core of Being with a rig of words, how long have I been drilling? Surely I am searching for the voices of the stars, but do I know what I will find?

If nothing
is possible,
then everything
is
miraculous.

GRANTS PASS

Hidden in a mystical chamber somewhere in the center of the universe, there are seven wheels of
fortune, it is rumored, all lined up on the same axle,
turning at different speeds and in reversible directions. A single, narrow slit passes from the
center to the rim of each wheel so that as proba-
bility has its say, there will occasionally in eternity be moments when all seven slits line up,
exposing a rare shock of light, a sudden *burst* of
quintessential illumination, setting off a parting of a
Red Sea or two. The very improbability of an
event itself sets up the possibility of its occur-
ring. The story goes in search of itself. Chas-
ing everyone every which way until someone has
fallen into its every rift and hollow and climbed
its every peak, the story itself sees to its
own rendering. The words themselves make
sure there's someone there to speak them.
The event is itself the architect of circumstances leading to itself. The story is the
artist of itself. It's all a matter of timing.
Timing full of grace, timing most exquisite,
great wonders there portray; yet at the
heart of grace, find blunders...at the
heart of blunders, grace.

As a compelling exercise in acclimating to the condition of responsibility, the syllabus for this study session recommends everybody, in or around the twenty-seventh year, try revealing oneself to Rabbi Liebowitz as the savior of the world. I blew my cover in Rabbi Liebowitz's office in nineteen hundred and seventy-one, just over the county line in Baltimore's northwest suburbs. I drew his tears. (He thought I was mad...but still, a Rabbi's tears are a Rabbi's tears.) That earned me points. And our tears mingled. (That doubled my points.) Outside, the handpicked trees and shrubs that pander to suburban fancy were bristling with the colors of early autumn. The air was crisp. The sky was soft azure. When I stepped out of the Rabbi's office door, tears had hardened to anger and softened to resolve. My brief respite in my parents' home had reached its end. It was time for me to leave...to head west.

Tisha watched from her nesting place on the green-and-black-striped afghan that was neatly folded in the pillowed lap of the big, wooden-framed armchair that Dad and I had carried up from the basement and put next to my bed. Her little white-and-brown snout was buried in her dainty paws...and the delicate intrusion of her soft, light brown, floppy ears in our exchange of glances deepened the omniscience in her brown-eyed watchfulness as I hastily threw my things together. I stroked her silky cheek, backed out of the room into the hall, left a note on the kitchen table, went to the cellar, exited cautiously out the cellar door and headed north to Middletown, Connecticut. If I didn't find God in Connecticut, I'd take a bus to Pittsburgh, hunt up a nun I'd met at St. John's seven years earlier, and then hitchhike the rest of the way to Oregon.

I'd never been on the west coast before so I fed on the forms and colors of the journey like a baby at the breast. The mountains were petrified echos of antediluvian thunder; they were the feet of the endless stretch of western sky and the plains were memories of their passing long ago. Soft pinks, hushed oranges, browns, yellows, mingled with fades and shades of green and fields of golden, swaying grass and sun-baked mounds and walls of rock and clay, and then sprang without a warning the harsh surprise of salt, white desert. Hidden slyly on the other side of throngs of crowded, dancing hosts of hills and valleys sprang the salt, white desert, pushing west. Paula and I had been separated a year when I entered the land enchanted by the giant trees.

Half of forty acres climb the side of a small, wooded mountain in Selma, just north of Grants Pass in Oregon's southwest corner. Halfway up the mountain, with a rickety crate stacked neatly with paperback books and a drawing pad lying open on a thin, cotton batting mattress, Paula lived. In a tiny hovel dug out of the ground, covered with gray, weathered boards, piled around with rocks and heavy branches, cut straight and even, packed with dirt and clay, a wooden pallet for the floor, she lived, while down below, on the edge of a small, elvish clearing, in among some thinning birch, her house of logs was rising. When I arrived in Selma, Paula was in Eugene, a hundred miles to the north, selling her pen-and-ink drawings at the university. I stayed the night in Selma in a small, square, shingled goat shack with a sloping flat roof, a wood-burning stove and the goat outside and, as Paula wasn't expected back for several days, I left for Eugene in the morning.

Poking through grated openings in the concrete crust of the plaza outside of the student union where I was told Paula did most of her selling, a company of fledgling firs, whispering secrets to the bright midday sun watched as I drew near. Through a line of glass doors separating the plaza from a sprawling complex of low, granite buildings that housed the union, I entered an empty mall with window walls which in a moment would erupt with a rampaging student horde hastening to the next outposts in the appointed rounds of the day. In the rush I stopped a coed, lugging a knapsack by a single strap slung over her right shoulder, and was promptly told that Paula had been staying on the couch in her parlor and had left that morning to head back to Selma.

Trying not to think about the odds against my coming across this information at all, let alone having it come fountaining forth in casual response to my first casual probe into

Paula's whereabouts...trying to make a habit of accepting collect calls from other worlds without asking what the charges were for the first three minutes, I quietly ascribed the event to my newly burgeoning paranormal senses and spent the night in an upper bunk in a crashing room in a Mormon hostel run by some awkward young missionaries trying out their zeal in Eugene. They fed you oatmeal in the morning at seven-thirty sharp, even if you hadn't attended the religious service the night before, then sent you on your way. I arrived back in Selma before noon, just in time to crowd with everyone into the back of an old black van bound for Grants Pass.

Heavily bearded, dark and heavyset, with a full, indomitable face and manner, Jonathan didn't build cabins but sculpted them. He drove the twenty or so miles into Grants Pass. I sat behind him next to Carolyn, on a mattress propped up against the side panel, and grasped at glimpses of rocky, pine-covered hills and dwarfed mountains that peeked through the windshield and front-door windows of the otherwise windowless vehicle as it chugged along its way.

Carolyn was fair and slim. Her face was soft and winsome and suggested the appetite for transience that had her making the five-hundred-mile trek to Berkeley and back almost weekly. Her hair was light and braided into pigtails that rested on the shoulders of a cotton jersey with a blue-aster print. She wore a long skirt and sat cross-legged between me and the driver's seat.

Jeremy sat in the passenger seat next to Jonathan, with his elbow resting out the window. He was slight and boyish, withdrawn, almost submissive. Paula sat at the front of the cargo space, facing the back of the van, her hair prancing with curls, her terse good looks and godliness assumed. Laura, Paula's sister, younger by four years, taller by half a foot, big with Jonathan's seed, sat beside her.

There was nothing unusual about our arrival that day in Grants Pass, Oregon. There was nothing unusual, before addressing the business of the day, about taking a few minutes to dawdle on the stone steps of the Grants Pass Post Office, just around the corner from where we had just parked. Before being greeted by a hireling in the service of the local police department who kindly solicited identification from the three women and kindly whisked Laura off to jail when she failed to produce any, there were a few not-unusual minutes to dawdle and arrange our proceedings. As business interests took a sudden turn in favor of Laura's rescue, our modest regiment hastened toward an ill-prepared assault on the bastion of Grants Pass law enforcement.

If Jonathan had allowed some discussion of strategy, I would haved stayed with the strike force. But as it was, he didn't.

He doggedly didn't. So I deserted. As we got closer and closer to the stationhouse, I fell farther and farther back in the ranks. When this storming flock of determined warriors disappeared into the jai/house, I was sitting on the curb in front of the library across the street.

Making unsubtle references to dirt and litter and me in the gutter, an energetic man in a light brown suit and green tie, his face gaunt and tight, in his maybe early thirties, swinging a leather briefcase like a child off to school in the morning, took a generous moment out of his day to personally welcome me to Grants Pass.

I raged. Pounding my fist on the curb, I raged. Screaming this was my blankety Earth no more or less than his and I'd park my blankety butt wherever the blankety butt I saw fit, I raged.

As though he'd played no part in my disturbance, this strange man crouched suddenly close to me, asking me what was wrong with an alarming intensity and concern that left me disarmed and disoriented just enough so that I found myself explaining to him, almost against my will, the circumstances that constrained us.

With impeccable attention, the man listened. An ember of fire appeared in his eyes and in its glow, like Odysseus throwing off his beggar's disguise in *the great hall* of his castle in Ithaca, his face took form. When he flew into the police station, he was the flight of Odysseus's first pitiless arrow that caught Antinoös beneath the chin, even with the cup in his fingers, even with the wine at his lips, pierced his throat all the way up to the feathers and filled his gullet and his nostrils with the unexpected wine of life's last blood. He stormed out of the police station dragging Paula's sister by the arm, making quite a ruckus and throwing threats around like confetti.

In a spacious office on the ground floor of a large white house with yellow trim, only a short walk from the scene of an impassioned and unexpected rescue in Oregon's southwest corner, the light from four tall windows, filled with sky of laughing blue and cotton clouds sculpted softly into pillows piled up high like mountains for the sky to rest its head...light from windows crystal clean that hung no curtains, glanced off of polished hardwood floors that wore no rugs and flashed on high, white plaster walls that hung no hooks or nails and bore no frames. Next to a tall gray filing cabinet, on a golden oaken desk, perched two dark socks that wore no shoes and warmed two feet belonging to the unexpected and impassioned rescuer, casually slouched, rhythmically rocking on the back legs of a tall, purple vinyl chair.

49

His name was Robinson; he was a lawyer. At his invitation we had followed him back to his office, and now we all sat in metal folding chairs gathered around his desk. The scarcity of furnishings in his office suggested, as might easily have been the case, that he was opening a new practice and we had just been treated to a grand-opening special.

Can it be appropriate to ask someone who has just victoriously laid single hand-ed siege to an entire police station in your behalf about their motives for doing it? Yet Jonathan, as though there were some pernicious plot...some sinis-ter seed waiting to be uncovered, became fixated on trying to expose an impurity in the rescuer. Un-checked, Jonathan's query easily took center stage and would have held the spot exclusively but for my objections, which continued unsupported, even on the ride back to Selma, until I finally, in short words, demanded that the truck be stopped. I hopped out with my sleeping bag, knapsack and a black velour clothing bag I'd sewn from a coat I found in *The Free Box* in front of The Old Cambridge Baptist Church in Harvard Square, its broad white strap slung over the shoulder of my green army jacket, and headed south to Berkeley and Molly, who would inhabit the next eleven years of my life.

Dear Mom and Dad,
   I promise never to try revealing myself to Rabbi Liebowitz again. I will come home for a visit when you promise to try thinking I am not crazy. ♡M

THE POINT OF REF-
ERENCE FROM WHICH
WHOLENESS IS PER-
CEIVED IS FUTURE-BORN.
IT LIVES JUST PAST
THE OTHER SIDE OF
CHILDHOOD'S *EYES.*
UNTIL THE JOURNEY
TO THE OTHER SIDE
OF CHILDHOOD IS
TAKEN, *THE CHILD IS
CLOSER TO US THAN
WE ARE TO OURSELVES*
— MAKING *THE
CHILD THE KEEPER
OF THE GATE* — SO
ONLY BY *THE CHILD'S
GRACE IS THE ENTRY
INTO WHOLENESS
GRANTED.* THE
CHILD KNOWS NOTH-
ING OF ITS POWER
AND THEREIN LIES
ITS POWER — IN
INNOCENCE AND
WONDER.

50

"Let us then try
what Love can do...
Force may subdue
but Love gains:
And he
that forgives
first, wins
the
Laurel."
William Penn

PREMiSE

War is dishonest. Everything
having to do with war is dishonest.
And as the nature of a dishonesty
will compound upon itself and the interest it accrues
until it reaches its own critical mass and explodes,
so will the very thought of war, left to its own
devices, eventually trigger the mechanism of its
own pathology, compounding upon its own rationality,
feeding off of its own poisonous mentality, leading
at last, without recourse, to the obscenity of war
itself. The thought of war is itself sufficient to
see to its own rendering. The balance rests in
the power of an honest thought. This is as it
should be. On currents of feeling, we drift and
collide. On wings of thought, we soar.

An enemy is a convenience at best—
at worst a luxury item...and is
always a way of avoiding looking
at something disagreeable in ourselves. Wars
aren't fought against enemies but against the
sickness, the emptiness and the loneliness bred
into us by the inadequacy of our own cultural

premises. *There is no enemy*... but only an ideo-
logical paucity or dysfunction in the concept of
our interplay. There is only a lack—something
amiss inside of us—a hole in the boat—and as
we grapple with each other, the boat sinks.
Jesus wasn't making a casual suggestion when
he said to love our enemies. He was plugging
up the hole. He was pointing to the inward
trek, urging us onto the path of it and offering
illumination along the way. He was helping us
clear a hurdle in the corridor leading to the ultimate sanctuary and natural residence of the
spirit—the habitat of angels—the smithy where
swords are beaten into ploughshares—the trea-
sure room in the heart where the jewel of peace
is kept. Peace is like love. You can't negotiate
it or coerce it into being. Interludes between
wars can be negotiated and coerced into being,
but not peace. Peace itself can only be created
—and it can only be created with imagination
rooted in sound spiritual principles (loving
your enemy is a good one). The human spirit
feeds on opposition as does creation itself, and
when we fail to cultivate that opposition creative-
ly, we invariably end up satisfying this treacherous appetite by creating enemies...by degrading
and provoking each other. It's just the way we
are. Create a provocative and interesting peace or
inherit war by default. That's the law.

In everyone, we see ourselves. Even
in every terrorist act we see re-
flections of our own hidden desper-
ation, as in every act of love we see a rendering
of our own hidden softness. With every refusal

to pass judgment on circumstances that tempt us with too easy condemnation or even too easy praise, we give heart and sway to the cause of peace.

There is a need for opposition, and nature has never been sparing in its willingness to provide for the need. Without opposition there is no drama and without drama there is no life. Our choice is simply between good theatre and bad. Good theatre embraces opposition as an exponent of natural process. Bad theatre rejects opposition and tries to eliminate it. Art is the best ally of good theatre. War is the best ally of bad. The genius of the circle lies in an architecture that embraces opposition by its very nature, making it our best art teacher. The circle lives. In nature, it lives. It guides the journey that introduces art to itself and in so doing, produces wonder as though it were some residue given off in processing the matters of life heartfully and mindfully. Love your enemy. If he has no land, make a land for him. If he has no city, build one for him. If he hates you, take off your shirt and work beside him and bring enough food with you for his children...and don't give the food as though it came from you. Because it doesn't. Let your sweat mingle. And your tears. Not your blood.

deas are the children
of conscious life. When consciousness
stops producing offspring, its lineage,
like any strain, dies out.

IDEAS

There is a natural protective device built into us that numbs us to a tone that's held too long. I was visiting a first-grade classroom at an alternative school in Cambridgeport down by the Charles River when I decided this was most likely the case. The children's attentions were turned in every direction but to the sound of the teacher's voice. It must be possible to tire of hearing the voice of even the most wondrous of teachers.

After the class was over, I asked the teacher if he thought it might be a good idea to invite one of the children to be his voice for him. A child who liked the idea could stand on a desk next to him. He could whisper his lesson into the child's ear and the child could repeat what she or he heard, contesting things, confusing things, adding and refusing things, refining and untying and misusing things all according to the mood...like a theatrical script. Different voices and especially the voices of their peers might not only make it easier for the children to listen, but it might improve their attitude toward learning as well. A lesson could become a dramatic performance to charge the children's memories and ignite their learning lives with the electricity of a real event. Fun is fun.

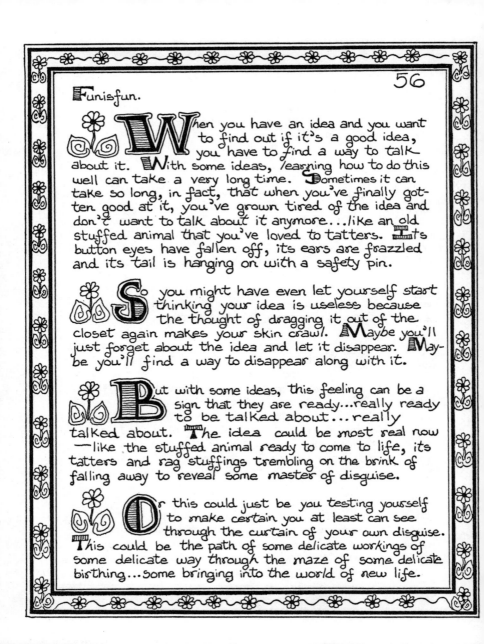

Funisfun.

When you have an idea and you want to find out if it's a good idea, you have to find a way to talk about it. **W**ith some ideas, learning how to do this well can take a very long time. **S**ometimes it can take so long, in fact, that when you've finally gotten good at it, you've grown tired of the idea and don't want to talk about it anymore...like an old stuffed animal that you've loved to tatters. **I**ts button eyes have fallen off, its ears are frazzled and its tail is hanging on with a safety pin.

So you might have even let yourself start thinking your idea is useless because the thought of dragging it out of the closet again makes your skin crawl. **M**aybe you'll just forget about the idea and let it disappear. **M**aybe you'll find a way to disappear along with it.

But with some ideas, this feeling can be a sign that they are ready...really ready to be talked about...really talked about. **T**he idea could be most real now —like the stuffed animal ready to come to life, its tatters and rag stuffings trembling on the brink of falling away to reveal some master of disguise.

Or this could just be you testing yourself to make certain you at least can see through the curtain of your own disguise. **T**his could be the path of some delicate workings of some delicate way through the maze of some delicate birthing...some bringing into the world of new life.

This is one reason why it helps to search for different voices inside of ourselves. **L**ooking for new voices by turning down the volume on the old ones or even turning them completely off to see what shows up to take their place...finding new and unexpected ways to frame a notion to make it eager and interesting again where it may have grown old and haggard to you, can make all the difference.

Perhaps it's true that I'm only saying all of this as a warning to myself not to let my own ears grow indifferent to the sound of my own voice, heavy with the wording of my own idea that weighs on me like a ton of tears and follows me like an albatross out to the open sea. **I**deas are much more valuable than platinum or gold and the weight of them is just the ripening fruit pulling down on the branches of my thoughts. **I**deas are the fuel to drive the vision...and without a vision to drive our hearts and call us out from hiding, we are only barely human.

Then take to words as eagles take to flight. **G**rasp for words as last breaths gasp for life. **W**hat thought will leave us to our peace until its piece is said? **W**hat page left blank, what word or line unwritten, what pen left idle will let us pass into the land where bubbles never pop...where love is never lost and only found?

"I am the wilderness,"
says the spirit of creation.
"The whole universe is wilderness
territory because that is the
nature of my body. How long
can you live and how shall I
be unto you when my body and
my peace are broken?"

THE BREATH of the EARTH

Speaking, whether it is with voice or
pen, is like building a house in the
wilderness, because the silence is the
wilderness, body of all that is sacred...but whereas
a house rests on the Earth, words rest on the
silence. When we forget to honor the Earth in the
way we design and build a house, the house
becomes an ongoing barrier between ourselves
and the whole body of nature. When we remember to honor the Earth in the way we build a
house, the house becomes our most intimate link
with nature.

The same thing is true of our words.
When we forget to honor the silence
in the way we form our words, our
voice and our pen become barriers between ourselves and the body of all that is sacred. When
we remember to honor the silence in the way we
form our words, the heartbeat of the silence
mingles with the sound of our voice and the
scrawl of our pen becomes easily mistaken for a
comet streaking across a midnight sky.

Words emerge out of the silence like we emerge from the Earth. Silence is the language of the wilderness and the wilderness is the breath of the Earth. The wilderness process is what keeps the planet alive and breathing. The destiny of civilization isn't to desecrate and draw the lifeblood out of the wilderness — to shadow and smother its lifeforce — to parcel off the wilderness and sell it by the pound. Our destiny is to function as a vital organ in the exuberant life of the wilderness body — to unfold like a wilderness blossom — to honor the wholeness and wisdom of nature as the living embodiment of all that is sacred — to align with the planetary purpose of human beings which is rooted in stewardship. The true body and form of civilization live implicitly in the shape of our freedom. Our freedom is in our purpose.

The freedom of the heart is in beating. The freedom of the lungs is in breathing. The freedom of the mind is in questioning and seeking and finding. The freedom of the spirit is in loving, of hummingbirds is in humming, of bees is in buzzing and pollinating flowers. The freedom of a thing is in its service to the creation — in performing the function which nature had in mind for it from the beginning of time — and in every freedom, in every true act, the mystery and wonder of creation are revealed.

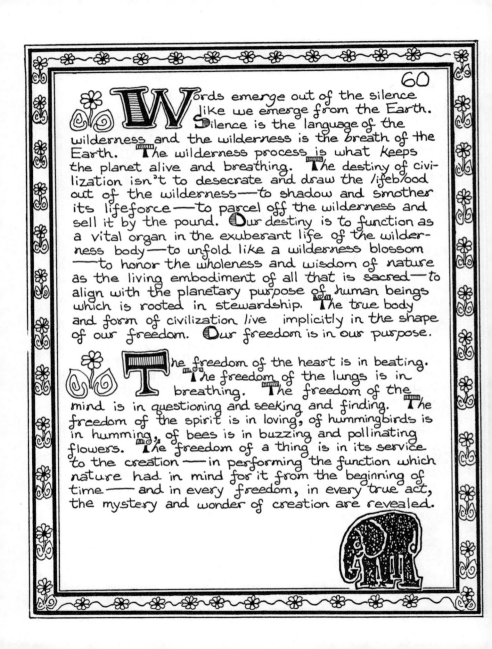

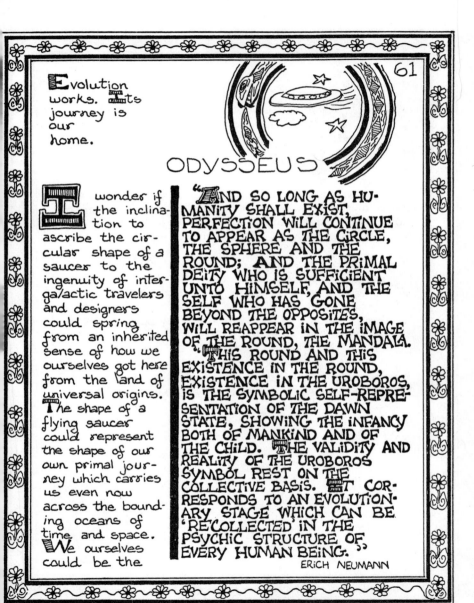

Evolution works. Its journey is our home.

ODYSSEUS

I wonder if the inclination to ascribe the circular shape of a saucer to the ingenuity of intergalactic travelers and designers could spring from an inherited sense of how we ourselves got here from the land of universal origins. The shape of a flying saucer could represent the shape of our own primal journey which carries us even now across the bounding oceans of time and space. We ourselves could be the

"And so long as humanity shall exist, perfection will continue to appear as the circle, the sphere and the round; and the primal deity who is sufficient unto himself, and the self who has gone beyond the opposites, will reappear in the image of the round, the mandala. This round and this existence in the round, existence in the uroboros, is the symbolic self-representation of the dawn state, showing the infancy both of mankind and of the child. The validity and reality of the uroboros symbol rest on the collective basis. It corresponds to an evolutionary stage which can be 'recollected' in the psychic structure of every human being."

ERICH NEUMANN

ones who haven't landed yet on Earth.

The whole notion of extraterrestrial contact could symbolize our aspiration toward the consummate bonding of ourselves with ourselves, of ourselves with each other, of ourselves with the Earth and the whole universe ...all of it. It could be a metaphor of bonding... of fusing the mystical and practical sides of creation into the minting of a single coin...into a picture of a logic that collaborates with the unfathomable....with the whole question of origins and of existence itself.

So perhaps we are drawn to the circle as we are drawn to the idea of a unified body of being. Perhaps we withdraw from the circle as we withdraw from touching something so deep inside of ourselves that it stings with the memory of primal wounds so deeply buried in the story of our race, we have forgotten them. Perhaps the gentle, glowing discus that hurls ever faithfully through the universe is the unseen sailing ship of Odysseus's perilous voyage home to reclaim his wife, his son and the lands of Ithaca. Perhaps we are Odysseus.

Two little people playing jumprope with a big chicken.

THE SMALL ROOM

It has recently been discovered that our immortal souls are manufactured on a tiny machine in a small room on the third floor of a rooming house somewhere in Pittsburgh. There is one small window in the room, and from it you can see forever. One of God's most important jobs is making certain every soul gets a glimpse out of the window before beginning its journey into the creation. That glimpse lives at the roots of every longing, so all you have to do is follow a longing to its roots and you will find yourself there again in a small room on the third floor of a rooming house somewhere in Pittsburgh, beyond the hint of want, standing next to God and looking out the window at forever.

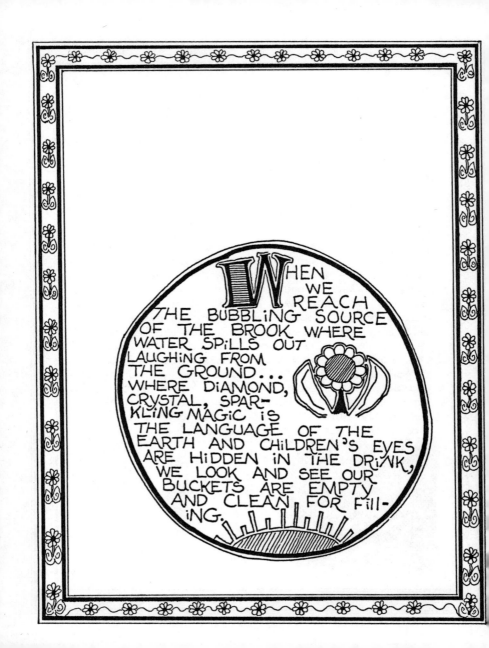

WHEN WE REACH THE BUBBLING SOURCE OF THE BROOK WHERE WATER SPILLS OUT LAUGHING FROM THE GROUND... WHERE DIAMOND, CRYSTAL, SPARKLING MAGIC IS THE LANGUAGE OF THE EARTH AND CHILDREN'S EYES ARE HIDDEN IN THE DRINK, WE LOOK AND SEE OUR BUCKETS ARE EMPTY AND CLEAN FOR FILLING.

As we learn to view human society more as a creative medium and less as an inherited condition, we cease to be victims of existing society's inequities and we become evolution's *little pathfinders*.

WETHERWEED
Introduction

What follows this introduction is a journey into the spirit of one person's visionary home on the Earth. Although this vision lives in what we would call the future, don't let its unmanifested condition fool you. It's at least as real as what we have here now manifested.

This visionary home is a little village of circles called

I'VE TRAVELED TO THE FUTURE LAND. FUTURE'S CHILDREN CALLED ME AND I ANSWERED. NOW I KNOW WHAT THERE AWAITS AND THERE MY SPIRIT DWELLS. BY ACCIDENT, I LEFT IT THERE. I'LL HAVE TO GET IT BACK. TO GET IT BACK, I WILL RETURN AND TAKE YOU THERE WITH ME. SO PACK YOUR THINGS BUT TRAVEL LIGHT. ONLY TAKE WHAT'S IN YOUR HEART. IT IS A NARROW ROAD TO START. BUT IT BROADENS, AND YOU PICK UP THINGS ALONG THE WAY.

Wetherweed (an extension of "We thee

wed "), so named to denote a condition of marriage between the village and the Earth. We consider the circle to be the wedding ring in the marriage. We also consider the circle to be the opening in the birthing canal of nature's body through which a new and unprecedented humanity comes to romp upon this precious soil.

The threats of nuclear and ecological holocaust and the emotional, ethical and economic impossibilities implicit in the arrangements of our civilization show us the folly of searching for personal security in isolation from each other. The focus on personal security places barely penetrable walls between us and has brought the Earth to the breaking edge of survival. There is only one security: caring for each other. Nature, in her wisdom, made it so we can't secure survival for ourselves but only for each other.

We are in the throes of a protracted adolescence which has now transmuted into a global cancer. If the situation goes untreated, the prognosis is obvious. The treatment is equally obvious. We are facing the need to leave behind us, once and for all, the architectures and forms of self-centered concerns in favor of global concerns.

The survival of the planet means, first and foremost, *the survival of the wilderness process that invents us, births us, nurtures and sustains us.* To survive, the wilderness process requires that civilization be reformed. Civilization has to learn how to integrate its body with the wilderness body not by violation but by enhancing nature in every possible way. We are all children of the wilderness, so to collect our final inheritance, our planetary identity, we have to return to the wilderness...to our place of origin. It's just the law of nature that we have to return to our starting place and complete the circle of our lives before we can collect the inheritance, because in the end the completed circle is the inheritance. Civilization's identity is in nature, not in its own fabrications. Disregarding nature disinherits us from nature, making us subject to nature's disregard, leaving us vulnerable to every kind of disaster and disease... because disregard breaks the circle of creation. This means we can't find nature and nature can't find us to help us, heal us and make us whole... because nature is *the unbroken circle.*

The wilderness is the fount of all life. It carried us and nurtured us as our mother and accompanied us as our sister in the infancy of our race. The wilderness is the firstborn of the Earth. Civilization is the second. The genealogical link between the two is the door into sanity.

The wilderness sprawls. *The sprawl* is the dance the wilderness does. *The sprawl* is the dance of preconscious life. And since the wilderness is the stage where civilization makes its appearance, the roots of civilization also reach into the soil of preconsciousness, so it's only natural that civilization would learn the wilderness dance first, just to try it out.

But the problem is, a sprawl doesn't know how to stop. Stopping just isn't designed into the anatomy of the thing. A sprawl will always sprawl some more. It is a dance that doesn't end...so where civilization and the wilderness meet, there cannot be a joining. There has to be a clash. This clash is where the wilderness is subdued and the spirit of the planet begins to unravel. Civilization and the wilderness can't both sprawl. One has to surrender that dance to the other.

The ability to break habits is an important characteristic of conscious life. The ability to stop one behavior and the ability to shift from one behavior over to another are both characteristic of consciousness. In fact, it could be that consciousness is born out of stopping and changing. So the roots of civilization reach into the soil of preconsciousness, but its branches, its aspiration and its destiny, reach into the conscious spheres. By surrendering the wilderness dance to the wilderness, civilization reaches for its own dance and its own destiny.

But the spirit needs a dance that doesn't end. The sprawl was one. A circle is another. A circle just goes on and on...round and round, never starting, never ending...and yet it stops. **A** circle stops. **B**ecause there is nothing more perfect than a circle for it to become, it stops when it becomes a circle. **A**nd where the endlessness of a sprawl has no form, the endlessness of a circle has a perfect form.

While the sprawl of civilization represents a continuing threat to the wilderness, the border of a circle doesn't threaten but guards and enhances what surrounds it. **L**ike a jewel in a sacred setting, it surrounds and embraces from within. **A** circle fuses with its setting. **I**t joins, by its own design, the sacred tapestry of natural balances whose golden threads weave the living fabric of the Earth. **R**espect for the immunity of unformalized, undeveloped lands, which belong by right to the fragile body of wilderness *beings*, becomes not only recommended by conscience but also enforced by design. **W**hen a trespass invades not only a trust but also invades an architectural statement, it is less likely to occur...and the architecture itself becomes a continuing teacher, an abiding teacher, a transgenerational teacher of the boundaries of integrity and trust.

The purpose of architecture isn't to enclose space but to liberate spirit. **T**he strategy of *circular collectivity* is to embrace the Earth, the cosmos and each other in one brief statement...and to formulate human closeness and cooperation into a *constant factor* without undermining the integrity of private space....to search for an architecture that fits the dimensions of the human aspiration like a sacred shoe. With attached housing running in a continuous circle surrounding and opening to a large domed enclosure, the integrity of individual housing units is secured by separating them from each other with alternating and attached greenhouses. The traditional isolation of private homes, which normally reduces our lives to plays plagued by a scarcity of roles and creative options, disappears with the placement of a simple door. The door that opens from each unit into the central dome could be a continuing call to adventure. Stepping through into the dome could be like stepping into a magical closet that opens to another dimension. Many of the restrictions we have to place on the free grazing rights of young children in wide-open spaces could be written off the books. In the space between the child, the family and the rest of the world, all our demons creep. The idea of a circle is to fill that space with creativity and love.

The healing and creative powers of circles have been known for a long time. Building villages of circles, living mandalas to heal the spirit and the Earth and tap the psychic roots of being, makes sense and deserves a try. Circles work. Circles last. Look how long things keep going round. Look how well the heavens stay in place. The universe thought up the idea of circles long ago and many people have learned to put them to good use.

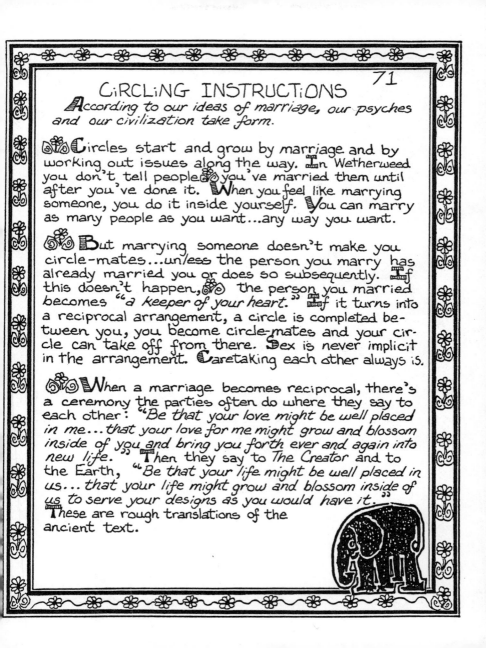

CiRCLiNG INSTRUCTiONS

According to our ideas of marriage, our psyches and our civilization take form.

Circles start and grow by marriage and by working out issues along the way. In Wetherweed you don't tell people you've married them until after you've done it. When you feel like marrying someone, you do it inside yourself. You can marry as many people as you want...any way you want.

But marrying someone doesn't make you circle-mates...unless the person you marry has already married you or does so subsequently. If this doesn't happen, the person you married becomes "*a keeper of your heart.*" If it turns into a reciprocal arrangement, a circle is completed between you, you become circle-mates and your circle can take off from there. Sex is never implicit in the arrangement. Caretaking each other always is.

When a marriage becomes reciprocal, there's a ceremony the parties often do where they say to each other: "*Be that your love might be well placed in me...that your love for me might grow and blossom inside of you and bring you forth ever and again into new life.*" Then they say to *The Creator* and to the Earth, "*Be that your life might be well placed in us...that your life might grow and blossom inside of us to serve your designs as you would have it.*" These are rough translations of the ancient text.

The way we hold each other is directly related to the way we hold the truth in our hearts... and the way we hold the truth in our hearts is directly related to whether the condition of our lives is more one of susceptibility to the generous supply of infirmities that plague our species or of receptivity to the feast set out before us.

THE ViSiON of WETHERWEED
Dream together or die alone.

Anyone can call a seminar on any book or subject for any time by putting a notice up on the S.I.B. (Sleep in Bunches) and Seminar Board next to the dining area in the center of the dome or by passing the word around. Sometimes there's a book you don't want to read alone. Sometimes you want to give a book or subject the added dimension that a seminar provides. Sometimes you do it for protection. (Some authors can *be* tyrants when they get you in their clutches, tempting and cajoling you, unraveling you until you don't know who you are anymore. To make a show of force, it's a good idea sometimes to bring an army with you.)

In Mead, as in most circles, *The Sleep In Bunches Department* is a popular place for winding down the day. Mead was the first circle completed in the Cordeville Cluster which guards the wilderness on the northwest border of Wetherweed. There are twenty-three hundred and forty-seven people in the village. There are two hundred and forty-seven in our cluster and thirty-six (including transient children) in Mead.

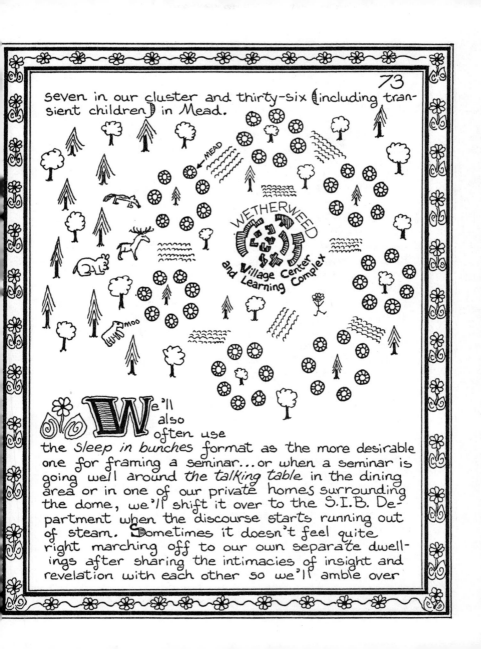

MEAD

WETHERWEED Village Center and Learning Complex

We'll also often use the *sleep in bunches* format as the more desirable one for framing a seminar... or when a seminar is going well around *the talking table* in the dining area or in one of our private homes surrounding the dome, we'll shift it over to the S.I.B. Department when the discourse starts running out of steam. Sometimes it doesn't feel quite right marching off to our own separate dwellings after sharing the intimacies of insight and revelation with each other so we'll amble over to the sleeping mat, climb into our sleeping bags and settle in for the night.

Every Meadian has a cubby with a sleeping bag, toothbrush and pillow in it over in S.I.B. so whenever an S.I.B. shift is called, we can make the move with the least possible distraction. Our S.I.B. Department is a giant sleeping mat in the middle of the dome, separated from the dining area by a green belt, a dense enclosure of leafy beings. The leafy beings have white spirits that help us *see* in the shadows of the evening. They create a feeling of closeness even in the middle of the wide-open expanse of the dome. In the starlight, after the pedestal lamps that hide in the greenery have been turned off, their leafy forms speak more softly than our kindest thoughts. They tune the undertones of discourse as though our thoughts were the strings of a harp. In our sleep they do the same thing for our dreams.

Each dwelling surrounding the dome has a window and a door opening inward to the common area. Through a window, through a door, through the greenage, an S.I.B. session looks like a campfire in the woods. The sight is a magnet to the spirit...and to the children who aren't staying overnight at *Canopy Hill*, the children's house in the center of *The Learning Complex*. The children will hide among the leaves and watch and listen in the silence of their own thoughts as a prelude to snuggling in with us on *The Slumberland Express*. We'll sense their presence and bait them with our dialogue. Much of the children's learning takes form as they hide in the greenery, listening and watching us.

Drawing the children out into the open eventually turns into a game... a kind of a cross between fishing and hide-and-seek. **W**e call it *interplay with the unseen child*, and it usually turns into telling jokes and stories and dimming the lights. **W**hen the children do come out into the open, it is a silent coming forth... like shadows stepping into bodies. **T**hey rarely speak. **S**ometimes they do, but it seems they get their fill of us in hiding. **F**ed full, they melt with us into the closeness of the evening. **W**e drop off to sleep like a litter of puppies, watching the stars through the crystal ceiling of the dome.

The children are very conscientious about splitting their time between Canopy Hill and their home circles. **C**anopy Hill is designated as the children's territory, though not in a restrictive sense. **C**anopy Hill is an integral part of the life of the village. **E**veryone spends time there, and many of us lived there while the first circles were being built.

So Canopy Hill is full of memories of the beginning. **E**very loft, every hidden stairway, every secret door and room, every nook, every cubicle and compartment, every slide and tunnel is a link with the first spirit that captured us. **W**e decided unanimously that the first thing we built would be for the children. **T**hat decision set the tone for our whole adventure. **W**e looked at each other differently after that, like we had done something right and had nothing to hide. But it was not unusual after that for us to look at each other and start laughing for no reason at all. That's how Canopy Hill got nicknamed *The Laughing Academy*.

There are seven circles in the Cordeville Cluster with an average of thirty-four people to a circle. We named our circle after Margaret Mead because of a story about Buckminster Fuller giving a lecture at *The Museum of Natural History* in New York City. He was running on and on as he was sometimes inclined to do. Margaret Mead raised her hand from the audience and when he called on her, she stood up and said, "Bucky, will you please shut up." The former civilization was masculine in nature. Wetherweed is feminine. That incident has become a symbol for us of the advance of the feminine in us and the retreat of the masculine.

To resist the expansion of population beyond a certain point (there was always some confusion about what that point should be, depending on how we decided to accommodate population in the central body of the village), we gave a great deal of thought to designing natural controls into the ethic, the organization and the structure of Wetherweed. We decided the best way to do this was by only allowing *inward* expansion. This decision was consistent with the pact we made with the Earth never to grow beyond the outer circle of the village. We call the pact *The*

Earth Charter. It says we'll crowd ourselves out with our own poor planning before overstepping boundaries conceived in good conscience. We're hoping the interplay of our principles with our architecture and our lives will help us to maintain a population honed to scale with the geography and the need. Natural controls were always the ideal.

"Art is prayer."

These three words are engraved in a big granite rock in the center of the village. The circle is, to us, a perfect work of art...a masterwork of creation...a portal of transit between the material and spiritual worlds. The circles of Wetherweed are a prayer to us. We live immersed in a prayer

"EXPERIENCE SHOWS THAT A VERY POPULOUS CITY CAN RARELY, IF EVER, BE WELL GOVERNED; SINCE ALL CITIES WHICH HAVE A REPUTATION FOR GOOD GOVERNMENT WILL HAVE A LIMIT OF POPULATION. FOR LAW IS ORDER AND GOOD LAW IS GOOD ORDER; BUT A VERY GREAT MULTITUDE CANNOT BE ORDERLY: TO INTRODUCE ORDER INTO THE UNLIMITED IS THE WORK OF A DIVINE POWER——OF SUCH A POWER AS HOLDS TOGETHER THE UNIVERSE. BEAUTY IS REALIZED IN NUMBER AND MAGNITUDE, AND THE STATE WHICH COMBINES MAGNITUDE WITH GOOD ORDER MUST NECESSARILY BE THE MOST BEAUTIFUL. TO THE SIZE OF STATES THERE IS A LIMIT, AS THERE IS TO OTHER THINGS, PLANTS, ANIMALS IMPLEMENTS; FOR NONE OF THESE RETAIN THEIR NATURAL POWER WHEN THEY ARE TOO LARGE OR TOO SMALL, BUT THEY EITHER WHOLLY LOSE THEIR NATURE OR ARE SPOILED."
ARISTOTLE, POLITICS

that goes so deep that saying grace before a meal seems strange to us. If living on the threshold of God doesn't keep population in line with natural design, nothing will. We call the rock *The Grounding Stone*.

Beside *The Grounding Stone*, a granite ledge rises slowly from the Earth. It reaches a height of five feet, then levels off and heads for *Canopy Hill*. It enters the children's house through a stone arch a short distance away. Where the ledge levels off is where *The Time Line* begins and it has just enough time to portray our *Creation Myth* before passing through the arch.

The Time Line is sculpted into the ledge. It begins with a raised circle that we call *The Before and The After*. Next comes a depressed circle that we call *The Sooner or Later*. The two circles collide and explode and become the universe.

The Time Line is done in painting and relief, and it weaves its way all through Canopy Hill. The universe changes into an ocean when a giant fish comes swimming through among the planets and the stars. (The way we explain it is that the fish represents *the idea of a fish*...and the introduction of the idea is what brings on the transformation.) The stars start changing into cells and joining together, coupling, clumping, lumping together until they've formed into a ball. The ball becomes distorted as though some disturbance was taking place inside of it. The disturbance becomes more and more pronounced until the ball blows up suddenly like a balloon, contracts and goes shooting off. (The way we explain it, some cells in the center of the ball have smothered and died and started decomposing...and the cells surrounding the decomposing material have started withdrawing from it, creating an inner cavity and then a channel leading back out to the ocean. When the channel is completed, the ocean rushes in, the warmer inner cells contract from the cold, increasing the volume of the cavity, drawing in more water and more water, stretching the innards out until they rebound like a blow-up balloon, the ocean is forced back out, the dead cells are ejected and the first excretory system, the first mouth, the first gullet, the first stomache, the first breath, the first heartbeat, the first circulatory system, the first gulp, the first flush toilet and jet propulsion are all invented in one fell swoop...making withdrawal from dead material the first conscious act. The same principle works with dead psychic material...only with psychic material, the channel opens inward to the ocean inside of us.)

The Time Line has fun with evolutionary fantasies before it moves into pre-history and history, paralleling different courses of events and suggesting relationships between them. We decided to keep The Time Line free of words to encourage inquiry among the children...and an oral tradition has actually grown around it. It's interesting how the absence of words here and the presence of words there will both serve the same purpose.

Before *circular collectivity* and *the collective village* took solid root on the Earth — before the idea of a *collective organism* was introduced convincingly on a planetary scale—evolution seemed to dead-end in technology. It just seemed to bottleneck in the contortions and machinations of the individual struggle to survive. All the genius and passion of evolutionary process—all of its scheming and conniving—just seemed to have gotten irrevocably entangled in the development of The Individual...and the nature of the individual's struggle to maintain life and limb in the context of those entanglements seemed to do nothing but deepen the entanglements. Multiplied by the populace, those entanglements made civilization into a black hole that fouled and nearly consumed the whole natural world.

The introduction of *circling* (courting and maintaining a circle) into the planetary scheme didn't lessen the power of the individual but unleashed it by untangling our interpersonal lives and making us more accessible to each other. For example, in group process we can call a silence for thinking about something by simply putting something on our heads. (We call it *crowning the soul*.) Asking for permission to speak isn't applicable in *circling*. We merely claim our natural right to speak by putting something on our heads...and whatever time is needed for thoughts to form and words to come is allotted. **W**e protect personal power ardently. **A**n audience surrendering its power to a speaker is considered irresponsible.

As it turns out, *circling* seems to be the equivalent of a mathematical operation, doing for people what summing does for numbers, the idea being to combine the members of a diverse conglomeration of relationships into a unified conglomeration of relationships so you can work with them more easily. **W**hat summing does is to create a nice, neat, manageable column out of a scattered collection of numbers. **T**hen it transforms them all, as if by magic, into a single number so you can pay for everything in one lump sum. **Y**et the column is still there and the full value of each of its members remains intact. **S**omehow, each member of a column of numbers retains its assets and at the same time surrenders its assets to the creation of an entirely new number...a whole new idea called *a sum*. **T**he discovery of summing introduced an exciting new freedom into our relationship with numbers, clearing the way for our adventure into higher mathematics. **C**ircling takes the idea of sharing and designs it intimately, architecturally, implicitly into the fabric of our lives. **I**t introduces a new freedom into our relationships with each other, clearing the way for our adventure into higher humanity. **T**he more we share, the less we need, the less we use and the more we have to give back to the Earth to heal its wounds.

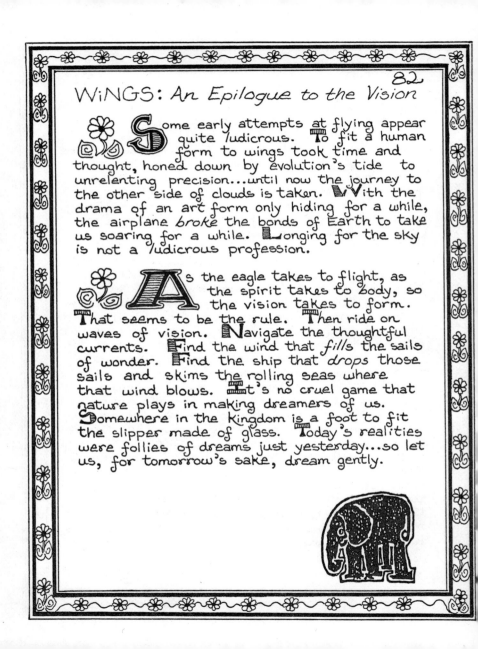

WiNGS: *An Epilogue to the Vision*

Some early attempts at flying appear quite *ludicrous*. To fit a human form to wings took time and thought, honed down by evolution's tide to unrelenting precision...until now the journey to the other side of clouds is taken. With the drama of an art form only hiding for a while, the airplane *broke* the bonds of Earth to take us soaring for a while. Longing for the sky is not a *ludicrous* profession.

As the eagle takes to flight, as the spirit takes to body, so the vision takes to form. That seems to be the rule. Then ride on waves of vision. Navigate the thoughtful currents. Find the wind that *fills* the sails of wonder. Find the ship that *drops* those sails and skims the rolling seas where that wind blows. It's no cruel game that nature plays in making dreamers of us. Somewhere in the kingdom is a foot to fit the slipper made of glass. Today's realities were follies of dreams just yesterday...so let us, for tomorrow's sake, dream gently.

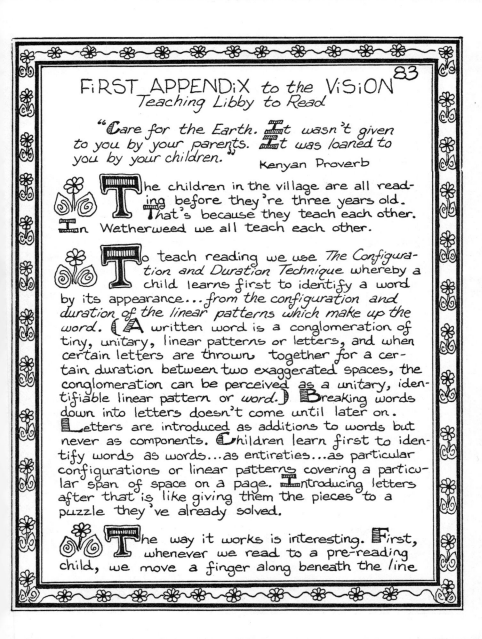

FiRST APPENDiX *to the* ViSiON
Teaching Libby to Read

"Care for the Earth. It wasn't given to you by your parents. It was loaned to you by your children."

Kenyan Proverb

The children in the village are all reading before they're three years old. That's because they teach each other. In Wetherweed we all teach each other.

To teach reading we use *The Configuration and Duration Technique* whereby a child learns first to identify a word by its appearance... *from the configuration and duration of the linear patterns which make up the word.* (A written word is a conglomeration of tiny, unitary, linear patterns or letters, and when certain letters are thrown together for a certain duration between two exaggerated spaces, the conglomeration can be perceived as a unitary, identifiable linear pattern or *word*.) Breaking words down into letters doesn't come until later on. Letters are introduced as additions to words but never as components. Children learn first to identify words as words...as entireties...as particular configurations or linear patterns covering a particular span of space on a page. Introducing letters after that is like giving them the pieces to a puzzle they've already solved.

The way it works is interesting. First, whenever we read to a pre-reading child, we move a finger along beneath the line we're reading. When the reading stops, the finger stops. The finger speeds up and slows down according to the reading so the children learn first to associate the act of reading with the actual temporal and spatial procession of the reading act.

Next, we choose some books that we're especially fond of and we read them over and over again until we find that we can stop in the middle of a sentence or stop just short of the last word or two in a sentence, flutter an expectant eyelash and hear our little preliterate saying what comes next as naturally as a drop plopping out of a leaky faucet.

Stopping short of the same word as it appears in different places on the same page, on different pages in the same book and in different books, and always making certain that we're pointing at the word we're saying while we're saying it, helps to reinforce the association between the linear pattern of a written word and the word itself. Pointing back and forth between different instances of the same word not only makes it clear that words are reusable but also helps to reinforce the association. Letters are never introduced to the children until they have a good repertoire of words. Libby's favorite word was *cucumber*.

We introduced letters into Libby's burgeoning system of wordage by taking a word she could identify (*oil*) and sticking a letter in front of it (*boil.... as in "boil us all in beezlenut oil"*). So the first thing Libby learned about letters was that when you put one in front of a word, it changes it into another word. She tried putting a "B" in front of "*cucumber*," but nobody knew what the word was.

Next we started giving more attention to other words starting with "B." Being careful never to point at letters in the middles of words helped to make certain that it was left entirely up to Libby to make the final leap from the idea of words to the idea of letters. She made the leap with the "B" in "*cucumber*". At first she was excited to find a "B" in the middle of her old friend. But then she looked up quizzically and gave the universe a suspicious and curious glance. The spelling chef had just ladled out to Libby her first serving of alphabet soup. There in her *bowl*, all of the words in all of the books were coming apart into so many little pieces, like the ingredients in a witch's brew, telling her that words don't come whole from the start... that they have to be put together... and the only things there are to put them together are letters...the spellbinding witchery of letters, of spelling lessons and the glue of her own imagination.

Approaching an entirety from different directions and perspectives seems to draw attention to its components in a natural way without separating them

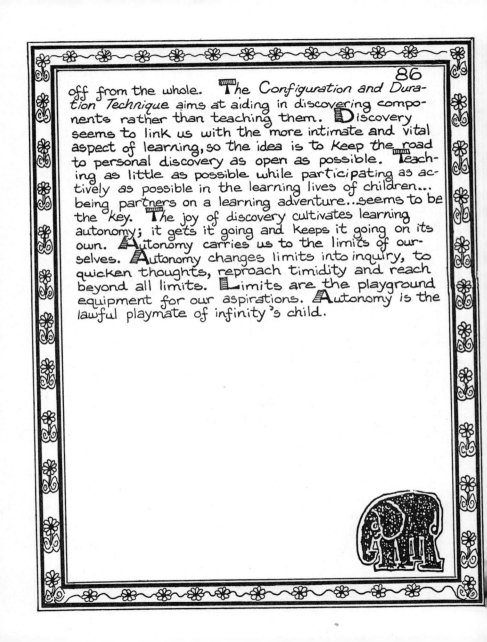

off from the whole. *The Configuration and Duration Technique* aims at aiding in discovering components rather than teaching them. Discovery seems to link us with the more intimate and vital aspect of learning, so the idea is to keep the road to personal discovery as open as possible. Teaching as little as possible while participating as actively as possible in the learning lives of children... being partners on a learning adventure...seems to be the key. The joy of discovery cultivates learning autonomy; it gets it going and keeps it going on its own. Autonomy carries us to the limits of ourselves. Autonomy changes limits into inquiry, to quicken thoughts, reproach timidity and reach beyond all limits. Limits are the playground equipment for our aspirations. Autonomy is the lawful playmate of infinity's child.

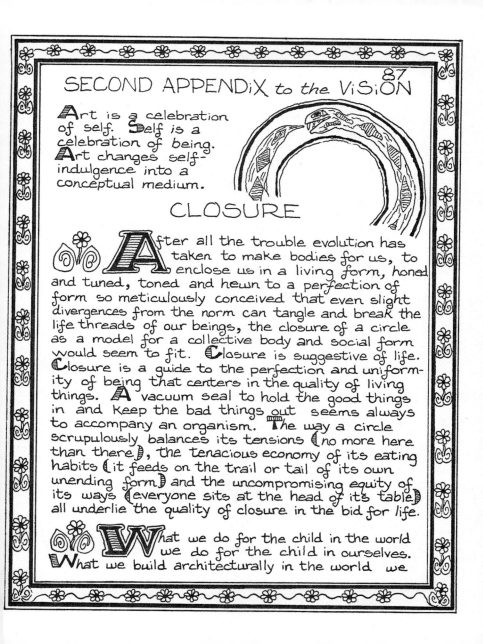

SECOND APPENDIX to the ViSiON

Art is a celebration of self. **S**elf is a celebration of being. **A**rt changes self-indulgence into a conceptual medium.

CLOSURE

After all the trouble evolution has taken to make bodies for us, to enclose us in a living form, honed and tuned, toned and hewn to a perfection of form so meticulously conceived that even slight divergences from the norm can tangle and break the life threads of our beings, the closure of a circle as a model for a collective body and social form would seem to fit. **C**losure is suggestive of life. **C**losure is a guide to the perfection and uniformity of being that centers in the quality of living things. **A** vacuum seal to hold the good things in and keep the bad things out seems always to accompany an organism. **T**he way a circle scrupulously balances its tensions (no more here than there), the tenacious economy of its eating habits (it feeds on the trail or tail of its own unending form) and the uncompromising equity of its ways (everyone sits at the head of its table) all underlie the quality of closure in the bid for life.

What we do for the child in the world we do for the child in ourselves. **W**hat we build architecturally in the world we awaken and establish psychically in ourselves. Building an inner dome and inward-opening door translates the architecture of inner consciousness into the framework of an outer world. Designing natural processes into structural concepts is designing life into life. Stepping through an inward-opening door into the enclosure of an inner dome is stepping out of the little box of the five or so percent of our brains that they say is all we get to use, into the other ninety-five percent. It's like a ski jump.

The circle is a blueprint for a theory of consciousness. The space contained within the boundary of the circle represents *totality*. Everything outside the circle represents *endless expanse*. Consciousness is the circle itself...the crossroad where *totality* and *endless expanse* meet and mingle with each other...where the *self* and *other* faces of being conduct their search for themselves in each other and for each other in themselves. Consciousness is the search for the balance of the two.

A circle is a buffer, a pillow to soften the shock of individual and separate existence in the middle of endless expanse. A circle is an inner face of being... a face that we can see. A circle is a workshop where the two infinities converge and make an image. *The Infinite* wants to see itself and so it makes an image.

Without a pillow...without the intermediary or stepping stone of some gentle circle being, the leap to infinity can be startling. Terror is only wonder without a pillow or a stepping stone...and as no stepping stone to get there is no stepping stone to get back, better to curl up in a little box of five percent with a good book. It makes sense.

The inward-opening door and the inward strategy then become a path leading outward in the world to meet infinity on terms better suited to surviving the encounter. A circle is a stepping stone outward in the world to see its needs more clearly and answer them more deeply. This is where we meet each other. In answering the needs of the Earth, we get to meet each other...at last...after all these years.

Circling transforms the parceling of land from something separating into something integrated with the whole. Circling transforms a private dwelling into a statement of collectivity and stewardship over lands guarded over by the circle...like approaching a whirlpool from your own angle to get drawn in and swirled around. Moving farther out in every direction, a merging with the stewardships of other circles occurs, moving on to meet the wilderness on its own terms, making interesting patterns and designs along the way.

Stepping through an inward-opening door into the totality of an inner circle loosens the reins that hold our thoughts back from their natural stride and pace. Totalities don't need categories, you see. Everything

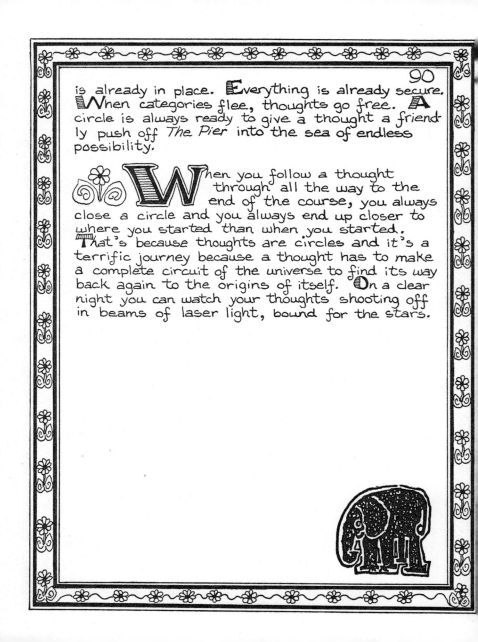

is already in place. Everything is already secure. When categories flee, thoughts go free. A circle is always ready to give a thought a friendly push off *The Pier* into the sea of endless possibility.

When you follow a thought through all the way to the end of the course, you always close a circle and you always end up closer to where you started than when you started. That's because thoughts are circles and it's a terrific journey because a thought has to make a complete circuit of the universe to find its way back again to the origins of itself. On a clear night you can watch your thoughts shooting off in beams of laser light, bound for the stars.

Genius is what happens when we find the intelligence to release intelligence. *Genius* is what's left when intelligence flies off. *Genius* is the complete absence of intelligence. That's the simplest thing of all.

DiALOGUE

Human beings have been known to by-pass questions in favor of answers not nearly as wonderful as the questions themselves. That's because we're fed information as answers when we're children, before we learn how to ask the questions. Our relationship with questions is left sorely deficient.

Answers aren't the answer. The dance that goes on between questions and answers is the answer. The answer is in our relationship with the question. Falling in love with the question is daring to become the answer. When we ask a question, we become disciples of our own asking. Until a question is asked we are prisoners of what we know waiting to be released by what we don't. Ask the questions. Ask them again and again. Ask them to the limits of themselves. In the asking—in deep asking—answers start appearing like fruit on a tree. A question is a tree. An answer is a fig or a plum. An answer is a wilderness blossom. The question is the wilderness itself. The purpose of answers isn't to eliminate questions but to deepen our relationship with questions...and so much of art is asking questions just to see what happens.

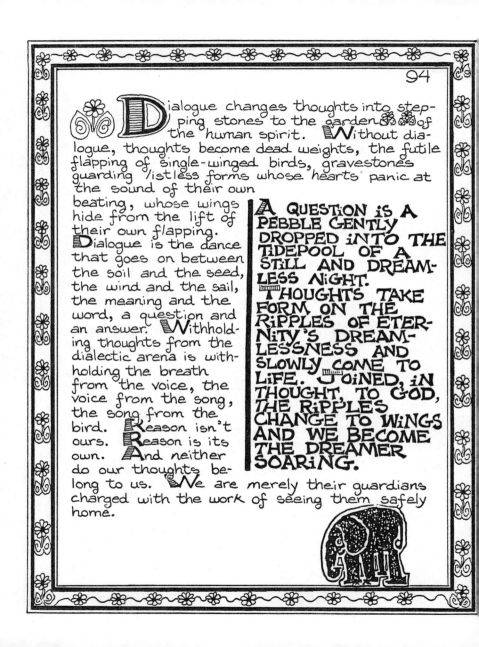

Dialogue changes thoughts into stepping stones to the garden of the human spirit. **W**ithout dialogue, thoughts become dead weights, the futile flapping of single-winged birds, gravestones guarding listless forms whose hearts panic at the sound of their own beating, whose wings hide from the lift of their own flapping. **D**ialogue is the dance that goes on between the soil and the seed, the wind and the sail, the meaning and the word, a question and an answer. **W**ithholding thoughts from the dialectic arena is withholding the breath from the voice, the voice from the song, the song from the bird. **R**eason isn't ours. **R**eason is its own. **A**nd neither do our thoughts belong to us. **W**e are merely their guardians charged with the work of seeing them safely home.

A QUESTION IS A PEBBLE GENTLY DROPPED INTO THE TIDEPOOL OF A STILL AND DREAMLESS NIGHT. THOUGHTS TAKE FORM ON THE RIPPLES OF ETERNITY'S DREAMLESSNESS AND SLOWLY COME TO LIFE. JOINED, IN THOUGHT, TO GOD, THE RIPPLES CHANGE TO WINGS AND WE BECOME THE DREAMER SOARING.

We test our ideals by seeing how well they translate into activism. Our ideals test us by seeing how well we translate into activists.

Wilderness is the primal stuff of being. It is Being itself. It is the universe unchained by the prisons of our formulas and expectations. Formulas and expectations themselves are only tiny wilderness creatures fading in and fading out of the cycles of natural life. They are only moss that grows on the shady side of our brains.

Wilderness is something more than material and more than spiritual. Wilderness is wilderness; it is absolutely itself. Materiality and spirituality both are only two more creatures the wilderness thought up, like lizards and giraffes, to fill the pockets of immensity. A nation unbounded, its identity is ultimately what we search for in ourselves.

WiLDERNESS: *The Unbounded Nation*
DECLARATiON OF NATURAL UNiTY

In the eyes of God on this 22nd day of September in the year one thousand, nine hundred and ninety-one A.D., to honor the ideals of freedom upon which are founded these *United States of America*, to utilize those freedoms to the limits of concerned and responsible discretion and to the limits of the capacity of those freedoms to accommodate the needs of the people by whom

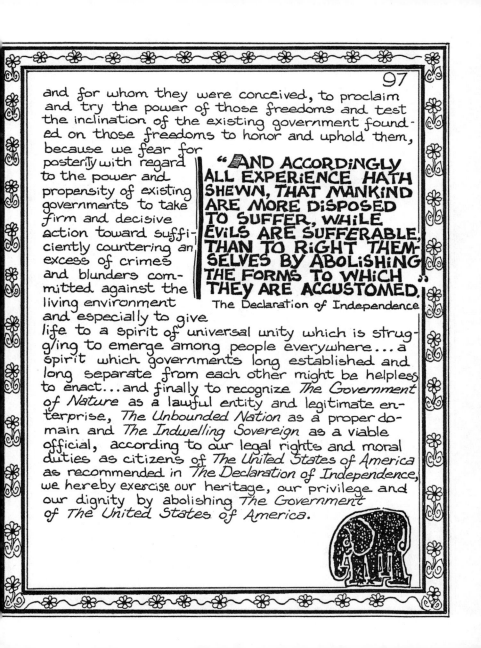

and for whom they were conceived, to proclaim and try the power of those freedoms and test the inclination of the existing government founded on those freedoms to honor and uphold them, because we fear for posterity with regard to the power and propensity of existing governments to take firm and decisive action toward sufficiently countering an excess of crimes and blunders committed against the living environment and especially to give

> "AND ACCORDINGLY ALL EXPERIENCE HATH SHEWN, THAT MANKIND ARE MORE DISPOSED TO SUFFER, WHILE EVILS ARE SUFFERABLE, THAN TO RIGHT THEMSELVES BY ABOLISHING THE FORMS TO WHICH THEY ARE ACCUSTOMED."
>
> The Declaration of Independence

life to a spirit of universal unity which is struggling to emerge among people everywhere... a spirit which governments long established and long separate from each other might be helpless to enact... and finally to recognize *The Government of Nature* as a lawful entity and legitimate enterprise, *The Unbounded Nation* as a proper domain and *The Indwelling Sovereign* as a viable official, according to our legal rights and moral duties as citizens of *The United States of America* as recommended in *The Declaration of Independence,* we hereby exercise our heritage, our privilege and our dignity by abolishing *The Government of The United States of America.*

DEFENDING HER RIGHT TO SING CHRISTMAS CAROLS ON BASTILLE DAY IN PITTSBURGH, A RENEGADE NUN IN JOGGING SHOES AND RED ARGYLE SOCKS WAS HEARD SAYING, "CHRISTMAS IS WHEN YOU FEEL IT IN YOUR HEART," AS THEY CARTED HER AWAY.

Speak I love you in ten thousand ways without using the words and the words will speak themselves without using the voice.

INVENTiON

If love didn't involve fear, it couldn't teach courage. **I**f love didn't address fear, it couldn't answer fear. **L**ove is one of the most general notions of all, which becomes one of the most specific when applied. **A**wareness of the existence of love doesn't mean we can love any more than awareness of the existence of electricity means we can flick a switch and have the lights come on. **F**irst we have to invent a switch. **W**e have to invent a wire, a generator and a light bulb. **B**efore we can have electric light, we have to invent an appropriate technology, and the same thing is true of love. **L**ove is invented. **Y**ou have to be an inventor. **L**ove is discovered. **Y**ou have to be an explorer. **L**ove is created. **Y**ou have to be an artist. **L**ove is the technology of the heart...the strategy of creation...the creation of the heart that unites the heart with creation itself. **I**t has something to do with putting something *there* that wasn't *there* before and then finding out it was *actually* there *all* along.

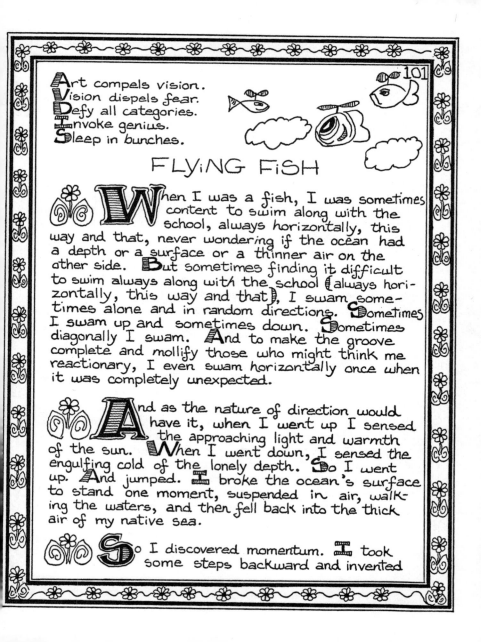

Art compels vision.
Vision dispels fear.
Defy all categories.
Invoke genius.
Sleep in bunches.

FLYiNG FiSH

When I was a fish, I was sometimes content to swim along with the school, always horizontally, this way and that, never wondering if the ocean had a depth or a surface or a thinner air on the other side. **B**ut sometimes finding it difficult to swim always along with the school (always horizontally, this way and that), I swam sometimes alone and in random directions. **S**ometimes I swam up and sometimes down. **S**ometimes diagonally I swam. **A**nd to make the groove complete and mollify those who might think me reactionary, I even swam horizontally once when it was completely unexpected.

And as the nature of direction would have it, when I went up I sensed the approaching light and warmth of the sun. **W**hen I went down, I sensed the engulfing cold of the lonely depth. **S**o I went up. **A**nd jumped. **I** broke the ocean's surface to stand one moment, suspended in air, walking the waters, and then fell back into the thick air of my native sea.

So I discovered momentum. **I** took some steps backward and invented the running start. I withdrew deeper and deeper into the thick air of my native sea and then made my move against the surface. Faster and faster against the surface. And I broke through. One time and another.

Then one day I happened on a depth I'd never known before and made a move from there. From there, I rushed the surface and jumped for the sun. From there, I shattered a stained-glass surface sea and caught God's wind by open fin. Alone in the air, alone in first flight, leaving oceans behind me and oceans before me, breathing hard in the air with the fear and the pain and the joy of virgin touch, I opened my fins, I saw that they were wings and my lungs first burned with fire.

❀ ❀ ❀ ❀

My patchwork coat was very active in the resistance. It was an old green army jacket. To make it warmer for hitchhiking the shorter northern route back to Boston in the middle of November, I covered it with patches. Deep browns...heavy Earth colors ...scarlet, beige, a very serious green and a patch of sky blue in the middle of the back all came out of *The Free Box* in People's Park in Berkeley. It was like sewing the Earth and the sky together so the fish couldn't get away anymore. I was wearing it when I met Molly. I also bought a pair of insulated hiking boots and some long underwear.

Hitchhiking out of Berkeley by way of University Avenue that day was like going on display on a department store shelf. **H**itchhikers lined the roads in clumps and bunches more frequently than lampposts for more than a mile leading to the expressway entrance down by the marina. **T**he interplay between hitchhiker and passing driver, the silent dialogue that gives hitchhiking its dignity and its metaphysics, was so diluted by this overabundance of contestants that I changed my mind about leaving Berkeley that day. **W**ith my sleeping bag, knapsack and black velour clothing bag, I walked back up University Avenue, ducked into the nearest gas station and gave an increasing intestinal pressure, which had been visiting and revisiting me with uncommon regularity throughout the morning, the attention it deserved.

There is a certain magic that hides in the bush and waits. **U**ntil the last penny is spent in the cause of wonder, it waits. **U**ntil what is known comes from nothing that is known, it waits. **A** brief morning rain had bathed the air and pried loose the pungent fragrance of the Berkeley Pines to dawdle with the senses. **T**he tingling haze was lifting. **A**n overcast of gray was showing fringes of white and breaks of blue when I entered the Crown Service Station on University at Alameda and asked for the men's room. **B**efore I noticed a bundle of neatly rolled bills lying on the cement floor just behind my right foot, ten minutes had passed. **A**nother two or three minutes passed before I dared to touch it.

Being destitute, I easily read the sight as markings carved out of a tree to show the way through the woods where the path is unclear. ▦ read the sight as tracks and traces left behind by the flawless force of will whose habit of confirming my course with magic was captivating me with wonder. **D**eciding whoever it was to lose was to lose and who-ever it was to find was to find, I took hold of my plunder, stuffed it in the pocket of my faded jeans still dropped and bunched around my ankles, and stood up. **T**o the one who had lost, it would be returned one day in another way, I decided as I pulled up my pants. **A**nd to the one who had found, it would be taken back many times over. ▦ walked nonchalantly out the door, a bit shaky in the knees.

IF OUR SPIRITS ARRIVE INTO OUR BODIES FROM BE-YOND THE FUTURE AND THE PAST—IF WE PASS THROUGH THE FUTURE AND THE PAST TO GET HERE, THEN RE-MEMBERING THE SIGHTS AND SOUNDS OF THE JOURNEY IS PIEC-ING TOGETHER THE STORY AND THE DESTINY OF OUR PLANET.

In Boonville, eighty miles to the north of Berkeley, in one of three long white house trailers cradled in the hollow of a soft grassy dell like three renegade chromosomes hiding from the genetic engineers, I slept with the rest of the men. **T**hree days earlier, a dollar and forty cents spent on breakfast, besides offering my gastric juices temporary employment and leaving me with twenty-eight dollars and sixty cents still in my pockets, had also left me stepping out of the door of a small diner a few blocks up from the Crown service station, directly into Eve Eden's path. My savings having been spent, my stomach having been empty and having never before found any money next to anyone's toilet, I had found it particularly easy to count my blessings and now I slept in the trailer next to hers. Huddled in my sleeping bag with the rest of the men strewn out across the thickly carpeted floor, I slept. The third trailer housed Reverend Moon, I was told, though I didn't see him there.

The earlier part of the evening I had spent disguised as a member of the audience in the lecture hall at the San Francisco headquarters of The Unification Church watching Eve Eden dutifully struggling against the sweet curtain of sleep to take an occasional note on Reverend Moon's talk in her little spiral notebook. Tilting forward slowly at the neck, she would collapse into a fall then catch herself and straighten, suddenly attentive with her pencil erect, again and again, as regular as a metronome set to keep time with *The Death March*.

After the lecture and a polite reception where you were permitted to go up to Reverend Moon and tell him how much you enjoyed his talk on "The Place of The Superior Man in The Evolutionary Scheme," two brand-new Dodge window vans full of people pulled away from their modest downtown skyscraper and, riding on wings of song, headed north to the Boonville retreat. Everyone was already up and out when I woke up the next morning, so making my way to the door of the trailer didn't mean stepping over outstretched bodies as making my way in had meant the night before.

Standing in the doorway, I paused a moment for a feast...a chilling morning's draught of crystal country air; outside, a circle formed for calisthenics. People sang and sang a singless list of of singless songs while I was dreaming hearts tuned in to speak without the silence breaking. I was dreaming villages all hidden in the hills and trees and houses set in circles, formed and dancing to a living pulse like strings of violins all tuned and ready for the symphony's first note, when someone stepped into the center of the circle and changed them into jumping jacks, all mindless, without words...still singing...jumping jacks in tune with Reverend Moon's "Creative Principle." Some faces turned to me and beckoned me to join, then turned back to the work at hand.

Down two metal steps to a small gravel landing just outside the trailer door I descended, then a tiny step attempted toward the circle didn't work. My molecules went flying up the hill. I clutched my knapsack, my sleeping bag and black velour sack.

Easing past the trailer, I took a step backward to retrieve a fleeing morsel of myself. Another backward step and another fleeing morsel was retrieved. Another step and another morsel. Another and another, backward rising to the grassy green top of the grassy green dell I crept, until the very moment when I might have ducked from view beyond the summit of the hill I noticed David frontward rising to the very door of me.

"I'm disappointed in you," he said to me without even knocking. David had taken a special interest in me because I was one of three people to receive his first talk introducing Reverend Moon's *Creative Principle* on the evening when Eve Eden had invited me to dinner. I shrugged and took another step backward without saying anything. David turned back down the hill and returned to whatever comes after jumping jacks in Reverend Moon's *Creative Principle*. I hitchhiked back to Berkeley.

Twenty dollars paid for five hundred copies each of two notecards I wrote and designed and had printed half on green card stock and half on blue, which I then took out onto the street and sold to people walking by. Molly didn't seem interested in buying a notecard. I gave her one for free in case she didn't have any money. She hugged me shyly. Sometimes the ground just suddenly appears beneath your feet.

BLUNDERiNG
TO THE LiMits
OF Blundering
itSELF, finally
Wins the
SyMPATHies of
THE plight it
self to grace
itSelf With Kindness.

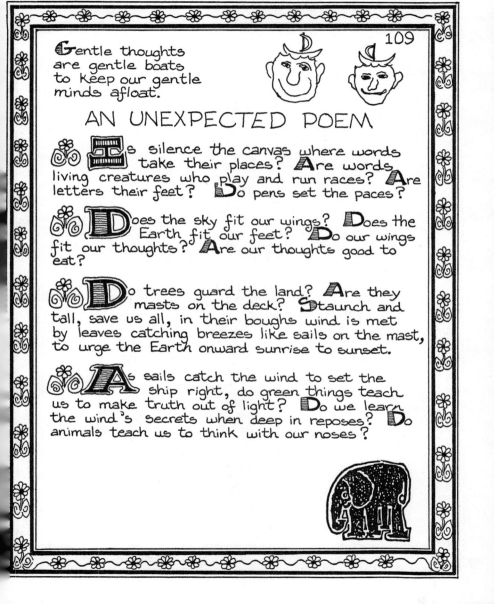

Gentle thoughts
are gentle boats
to keep our gentle
minds afloat.

AN UNEXPECTED POEM

Is silence the canvas where words take their places? Are words living creatures who play and run races? Are letters their feet? Do pens set the paces?

Does the sky fit our wings? Does the Earth fit our feet? Do our wings fit our thoughts? Are our thoughts good to eat?

Do trees guard the land? Are they masts on the deck? Staunch and tall, save us all, in their boughs wind is met by leaves catching breezes like sails on the mast, to urge the Earth onward sunrise to sunset.

As sails catch the wind to set the ship right, do green things teach us to make truth out of light? Do we learn the wind's secrets when deep in reposes? Do animals teach us to think with our noses?

I know I'm making art when I notice God beside me. We are only playmates in our portrait of the world. With every breath a brushstroke, with every pulse a glimmer in our eyes, together we are busy at our art. We are busy at our play.

WHY ARE THERE TREES?

AN EXCERPT FROM A RECENT CONVERSATION WiTH GOD

Me: Why are there trees?

God: There are trees because I find liberation in becoming trees. There are creatures, clouds and sky and stars and Earth because I find liberation in becoming creatures, clouds and sky and stars and Earth. There is you because I find liberation in becoming you. There is me because there is liberation in becoming...and *becoming* is who I am. *Becoming* is the heart of Being and *Being* is the groundwork of *Creation*. *Being* and *Becoming* tell the story of my liberation...

TEACH ME NOT TO BREAK THE LOCK. TEACH ME HOW TO FIND THE KEY. TEACH ME NOT TO FIND THE KEY. TEACH ME HOW TO ENTER iN. TEACH ME NOT TO ENTER iN. TEACH ME HOW TO BE WiTHiN. TEACH ME NOT TO BE WiTHiN. I AM WiTHiN. I AM.

and my liberation is the drama of the universe. The universe...the wilderness reaching from inside of you to out beyond the stars, is my unfolding.

MOLLY...An Introduction

I didn't know Molly was ready to go with me anywhere, even from the moment we met. I didn't know she'd already noticed me selling my writings on Telegraph Avenue and had already taken a decided interest in my presence in Berkeley, California. I didn't know she was walking down my side of the street only because I was there. I didn't know, when I stopped her in front of Shambhala books and used on her whatever line I was using at the time, that no line was necessary. I didn't know, when her crooked smile couldn't hide itself and she had to hug me to hide her embarrassment, that her rush of emotion had its source in a natural understanding of what had me on the street. I didn't know, while I stood waiting to see if words would come to play a part in connecting two lives, that for the moment silence was the only glue we'd get. I didn't know, when I tried walking away from her, that I wouldn't get very far. Being unable to think of any reason to turn away from her, I didn't. I backed...watching her watching me walking backward.

MOLLY TALKING ABOUT HERSELF

Love is
eternity giftwrapped.

The following portrait of Molly is pieced together from a letter to her brother, from some of her writings and from conversations. The words that follow are hers.

Molly: I wonder if people really believe that the shattering of illusions is a process of destroying hopes and dreams. For me it was important to find out simply what lasts and what doesn't. It's like building a dream through a process of elimination. Like when Michelangelo said you sculpt a horse by taking away everything that doesn't look like a horse. Getting rid of illusions is sculpting a dream. To be sculpting, you always have to be getting rid of something. You have to let crumble what crumbles and keep your eyes fixed on the form that's coming to be, even if you can't see it.

Watching Michael back away, I could feel him asking with his silence and the growing space between us if there was something I could say...if I could help him find a reason to come back. He was like a train leaving and coming into the station at the same time and I didn't know whether to hop on the departure with him or to wait and see if he was still coming in on the arrival. There was almost a whole block between us when

WALKING BACKWARD ISN'T JUST WALKING BACKWARD. IT'S ALSO MAKING ROOM FOR SOMETHING MORE TO HAPPEN—FOR A DEEPER REALITY TO SHOW ITSELF. HOLDING BACK, MUSTERING YOUR FORCES, GIVING COWARDICE ITS CHANCE TO HAVE A SAY WHERE BOLDNESS HAS ALREADY SPOKEN—MAKING SURE IT'S ALL OF YOU THERE AND NOTHING'S LEFT BEHIND IS MORE THAN A STRATEGY. IT'S WHAT MAKES SEAS OPEN TO LET YOU PASS THROUGH.

he stopped.

I had been in Berkeley three years before meeting Michael. I was there two years when I met a man wearing angel wings in the check-out line at the midnight supermarket on the corner of University and Grove. He was one behind me in the next line over. It was really important to talk to him and it was really important not to talk to him about his angel wings. If you ever really met any angels, you wouldn't want to talk to them about their wings...and you wouldn't want to leave them alone in the check-out line with nobody to talk to.

It was somewhat unsettling not having Michael know me right off like I knew him, but I resolved myself quickly and adjusted surprisingly well to the idea of being strangers just meeting each other for the first time. I didn't know from where or how I knew him, but I had recognized him the first time I saw him in his patchwork coat accosting people on Telegraph Avenue, even though he was turned away from me so all I could see of him was his back. There was a mysterious, deep familiarity drawing me to him...like we were both conspicuously out of the same fairy tale and ridiculously out of place in our lives.

❀   ❀   ❀   ❀

Dear Dick,
              Your letter and especially your poem really got me all excited. I fell right into a *that's my big brother* pride and it's fun. I didn't think you'd mind my showing your poem to everyone.

here. It was wonderful being able to say, "You wanna" see what my big brother wrote?" I'm trying to write my contribution to a magazine we're all working on and I'm driving myself up the wall trying to write it. I try avoiding it, and feel rotten about my lack of creativity. I see a flow coming but I haven't yet done quite enough to bring it to life. I try starting something but I always give up too fast. No persistence. No faith. Somewhere I'd like it all to be easier — who wouldn't? I'd rather not have to worry about survival. I guess I haven't really learned yet that creativity is the key to survival. I've always thought of it as an extracurricular type of thing. But it's really the essential focus. I sense you know that. I can feel it in you because the theme of your life has been a gargantuan odyssey, the specifics of which I don't know about and would like to.

You've always had big questions that needed big answers and I sense that when you're down and out it's because the answers aren't big enough. Am I right? I want to know you and what you're going through. That's why your poem was so important to me... because I feel you fooling around with the same territory that I fool around with in my life. What I know about that territory is that it can be really lonely finding answers by yourself. They make you lonely because they were meant to solve problems between people — and if they're not used the way they were meant to be used, the answers start becoming very heavy burdens on the person who knows them alone. That's why I said I've been driving myself up a wall—because I have a lot inside of me that I'm just developing the skills to share. I used to have to fantasize about sharing what's inside because I never knew how to actually do it.

You're very important to me. Writing to you creates a special tension that demands more from me. It's incredible, because I feel like you know me but it's somebody who I am not yet—and it's somebody I want to meet very badly. I almost feel you coming from the future, having already met me there, and you bring that person to a place where we can get a glimpse of each other. It has to do with your being my big brother but it's also much more than that. What's so exciting is knowing there really is a *me* out there who has become all the things that I want to become——and having a big brother who can serve as a liaison between me and me.

Molly

❁   ❁   ❁

All I know is at the beginning of seventh grade when I called Sister Mary Edward "Bird," like everyone else in the class, I almost gave myself a heart attack. You see, Sister Mary Edward never got back at anyone——and it seemed that by not getting back at people, she was activating a built-in mechanism where you automatically gave yourself a heart attack whenever you called her *Bird*. I thought I was lucky finding out about the mechanism so early in the school year. I figured it was just a matter of time before everyone else got theirs.

It used to really bother me that people would think of her as bumbling when I knew how powerful she was. I guess it was the old *Clark Kent Syndrome* where you can't reveal the person's true identity without ruining the story. This is not to say that given the opportunity, I wouldn't have ruined the story...because I would have. But she always made sure you never had enough proof to blow her cover.

You don't like someone just because she's a nun. That's probably why I did what I did on my first day of school at St. Robert Bellarmine's on the northwest side of Chicago. The year before, I had gone to the public school across the street from my house because they didn't have a kindergarten at the parochial school. So Sister Angela, besides being my first-grade teacher, was also my first nun.

It happened so fast that I don't know how it came about and it actually surprised me as much as anyone. All I remember is walking into the classroom with my mother. It was in the new wing and I was supposed to be very lucky to be in the first class that got to use it. The room was very large and was divided down the middle by a raised, tiered, marble fountain with a gold fish pond shaped like an elongated isosceles triangle running up and down the room. Fifty brand-new table-type desks filled one side of the room. The other side was more open, with large work tables, and doubled as the lunchroom for the entire wing.

Sister Angela was standing near the door welcoming each new arrival as pair after pair of mother and child entered the room. Seeing my mother was having some trouble getting me into the room, she came over to help calm my first-day anxieties. She looked real nice and acted real nice and stooped down and put her arm around me and was about to say something real nice but nobody ever found out what it was because I spit in her face.

You never know what it is or where it comes from until it just *happens* to you and you're finally or suddenly just stuck there feeling something that maybe you didn't even know you had hidden. It's like some moments are bulldozers that can in one dramatic sweep uproot and wipe out every notion, based on concept or expectation, of who you are or are supposed to be. And everything that used to be real to you is reduced down to absolutely nothing, confronting you convincingly with the necessity of starting to create, from the ground→up, a whole new idea of who you are.

It wouldn't have been so bad——everything would have made sense if only Mrs. Gladstone, my kindergarten teacher in the public school the year before, hadn't been so kind to me the day I forgot my clothespin for the pinwheels we were going to be making that day. When I realized I'd forgotten it and that I'd be late for school if I went back home to get it, I stood there frozen, looking at my house on the corner across the street, looking at the school, looking at my house, back and forth with me stuck in the middle, trying to decide if I was more scared of going in without my clothespin or of going home and coming back late without the crossing guard, without anybody holding the great fortress doors open for me and without a protective crowd of fellow kindergartners to accompany my own entrance into the classroom. I had never had to make a decision before. Terrified and with tears streaming down my face—all the children walking past me, eyeing curiously my distress as the last buzzer sounded—I found myself at last left all alone in the school yard. I didn't know anybody who had ever been late before. I didn't know what they did to you and I didn't think that being in kindergarten would get me off, especially since they were just accommodating me there until I entered the Catholic school the next year.

I didn't know really what an infidel was, but I knew from my mother that Mrs. Gladstone was one of them. If only she had been one of us. But she wasn't. My mother almost didn't send me to kindergarten because she wasn't. And not only was she not one of us, but she was getting old and was going to retire soon and then she was going to die and go to hell and I didn't know what to do about it. I stayed up nights trying to think up something I could say to her the next morning that wou'd save her soul, but whenever I imagined myself saying to her what I had thought up the night before, it always seemed wrong. I didn't know why it always seemed wrong, but it always did.

I had heard that infidels never liked talking to us because they were afraid of being converted. But still, I knew her life depended on it. And since I knew she wouldn't go near a nun or a priest on her own, I thought it was left up to me to get through to her before it was too late. But I didn't want her to be afraid of me so I did my best to stay away from her. So I wouldn't ruin my chances of winning her confidence one day when I thought up the right thing to say, I did my best to keep my Catholic presence from imposing on her. Learning how to get my coat quickly on and off by myself and learning how to hide all the trouble I had putting on my boots in winter so she wouldn't have to come over and help me like she did the other children, I managed to go through almost the entire year without having any contact with her ...until I came in late with my clothespin.

By entering through the cloakroom rather than the classroom, I had hoped to avoid Mrs. Gladstone, but there she was. At the other end of the long hall-like alcove, standing beyond the two rows of long wooden benches that lined the middle, sending the last of the children into the

classroom to play having just finished helping them put the last of their coats away, she
saw me appear through the far door crying.
Helpless in my anguish, left dutifully explaining
my tardiness alone with her there, awaiting my
sentence, I found myself suddenly the object of
compassionate and sympathetic amusement.

As I stood there overwhelmed and immo-
bilized, I watched her amusement sober into
a kind of astonishment that reversed my whole
field of vision and showed me my first window
into another world. While here I'd been
thinking all this time that she was staying
away from me because she didn't want to
get converted or get emotionally attached to
someone like me who wasn't going to have anything to do with her world anyway, now suddenly, through the window of her astonishment,
I was seeing myself the way she saw me...and
my great conspiracy to save her soul was
fading in the wake of my portrayal of a tragic
figure framed in the doorway of the cloakroom.

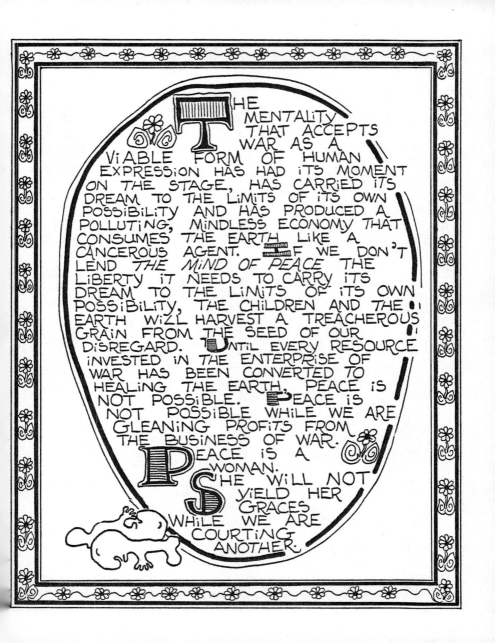

The mentality that accepts war as a viable form of human expression has had its moment on the stage, has carried its dream to the limits of its own possibility and has produced a polluting, mindless economy that consumes the earth like a cancerous agent. If we don't lend *the mind of peace* the liberty it needs to carry its dream to the limits of its own possibility, the children and the earth will harvest a treacherous grain from the seed of our disregard. Until every resource invested in the enterprise of war has been converted to healing the earth, peace is not possible. Peace is not possible while we are gleaning profits from the business of war. Peace is a woman. She will not yield her graces while we are courting another.

"Pain is just
the plow
to turn
the soil
of the
soul."
The IGSF

AFTERMATH

"Michael!" A tenor of distress in a man's voice calling my name.

"Michael!" Do I have to answer? Do I have to leave my sleep? I won't get back. A fist is pounding on the door.

"Michael!" My eyes open. I glance up at the clock radio...the little Sony Dream Machine I'd gotten for me and Molly. It triggers memories. Everything triggers memories. It opens a trap door in my stomach into a dungeon of memories.

It's three-thirty in the morning. An unsettling dark. Throw off the blue comforter that Molly bought. Reach for the light string. It dangles in the middle of the room with Molly's little brass bell tied to the end. Feeling through the darkness like a thousand times before. Milking the air. The bell is gone. Molly took it with her when she left.

Pull on your pants. Pretend to care enough to hurry to the back door. The street is alive with flames. Pretend to care. Open the door. You have to open the door. The van is on fire.

"It's your van," John says. Amy is beside him. Her fragile face mirrors merciless bursts of flames. Her eyes are alight. The night is alive with flames. Shadows dancing with the flickering lights against the houses and the trees. I think the night is clear. I think the stars are out.

"You never listened to me. You never heard me," Molly had said. "You never loved me."

"It's not true," I had answered. I wondered, could it possibly be true? How could I have hurt her the way she said I did?

"Did you ever hurt me?" I had asked.

"I never hurt you," she said dispassionately. I welled up with anger.

She was sitting in Alan Gimble's mother's car. It was an old gray Buick. Alan had gotten it when his mother died. I slammed the door and walked away. I caught her foot in the door.

I walked back to the apartment and stood alone in the front room. Molly came charging in after me.

"I never hurt you," she screamed. Pounding

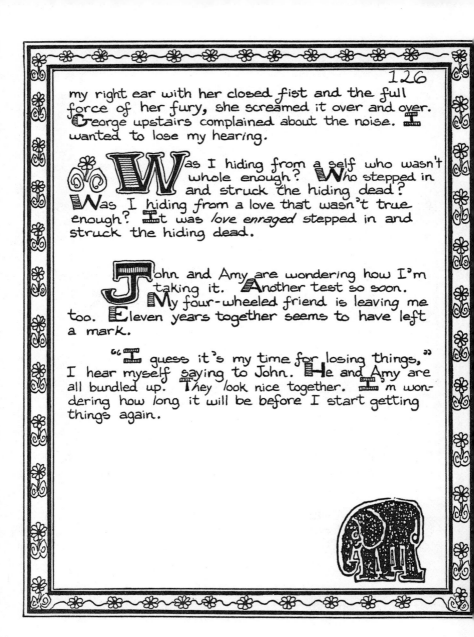

my right ear with her closed fist and the full force of her fury, she screamed it over and over. George upstairs complained about the noise. I wanted to lose my hearing.

Was I hiding from a self who wasn't whole enough? Who stepped in and struck the hiding dead? Was I hiding from a love that wasn't true enough? It was *love enraged* stepped in and struck the hiding dead.

John and Amy are wondering how I'm taking it. Another test so soon. My four-wheeled friend is leaving me too. Eleven years together seems to have left a mark.

"I guess it's my time for losing things," I hear myself saying to John. He and Amy are all bundled up. They look nice together. I'm wondering how long it will be before I start getting things again.

GENiUS iS THE NAKED

JOYCE GERRISH

SELF GOiNG THROUGH
OLD TRUNKS iN THE
ATTiC.

Is there a point where separation grows past the threshold of itself and becomes the unity of being? Is there a point where love grows past the threshold of itself and becomes a twinkle in the deep purple glaze of an endless night sky?

POiNT OF POWER
Childhood is the beginning and the end of the circle of our lives. Childhood is eternal.

It's unfortunate that we separate children into learning groups according to age and level of development because our identities take form according to how we learn. So if we find ourselves learning in exclusive groups, we end up relating with the world our whole lives as members of exclusive groups and only rarely as members of a unified humanity. The architecture of our learning lives becomes the architecture of our thoughts and of our interactions with the world.

We learn best what we are given a chance to teach and we teach best what we are still learning ourselves. Let the children teach each other in heterogeneous groups. This will make learning into an experience which is much more integrated with the company they keep throughout their lives. This will teach them to relate to the world with dignity, creativity and compassion. This will make their lives more of an immersion in learning...and when we are immersed in learning, all things become our teachers.

The thing with children is that *the entirety* of *being* is all they know, so until they learn otherwise, every utterance and gesture they make is a statement of the whole.....so in every utterance and gesture, the power of the whole resides. The language of entirety is what they know so that is what they teach. We don't teach language. We teach words. We put words to the language that already is there. Words are ours. Language is theirs. We have words but we have no language until we are in agreement with *the child*.

The integrity of a civilization lies in the quality, the texture and the dimensions of the learning environments it creates for its children. Investing in the child is working our way back to the smallest, wisest voice in ourselves where we are only whole...the point of entirety...the point of power where everything is the language of the whole. Tuning our ears to the smallest voices opens our lives to the greatest adventure. Nobody knows why it works that way; it just does. The voice of the child, when it finds itself again inside of us, is the source and power of all things. Finding this voice again closes the circle of creation and makes us whole.

*E*ven though we may grow uncomfortably familiar with incarnate status because there are so many of us around, it is very important that we not inflate the value of discarnate intelligence simply because it is not so commonplace. *A*nd it is especially important that we not deflate the value of our own wonderful blundering three-dimensional stupidity in favor of the glorious wisdoms of some ultradimensional know-it-alls. *F*amiliarity is death to wonder... like letting a pool stand too long still. *Y*et the life span of wonder is our natural birthright and its life span is forever. *T*his is why familiarity frightens us, and rightfully so, as we see our birthright being taken from us.

*S*o part of what I see in the channeling phenomenon is people fleeing from familiarity as from the death of wonder. *I* see people shaking their own limp spiritual bodies, trying to wake themselves up in the dead of spiritual winter so they won't freeze. *S*o I don't give too much credence to it...except for some of it.

IMAGiNARY FRiENDS
*S*ome fantasies are contrived.
*S*ome are discovered...like lost continents.

*U*ntil the first saucer landed publicly in the middle of June in 2003, there was no way anyone could have known how far beyond the limits of imagination reality can travel...that imagination is actually a finger of the subtle senses, a precise faculty for perceiving and touching the oceans of subtle

realities that lap at the shores of consciousness...that fantasy is a fabrication of real
messages received from the other side of our
Earthly sleep.

onathan Sparrow's first contact
with *The Intergalactic Space Feder-
ation* came in early February of 1985,
half a year after his second wife had left him.
He was still measuring his esteem in minus de-
grees, depending on the windchill factor, and was
in the middle of an extended study into the nu-
tritional value of emptiness when he stumbled
on the voice and agreed to let it have its say.

"Jonathan, your conscience carries you
away," it said.

his was true. He knew it was true.
The voice came from somewhere inside
of him and beyond him. Way beyond him.

"Come closer to the voices that sing the
songs that cleanse the heart of hurt and pain,"
it continued.

In light of his torment, this struck him
as a good idea. He picked up a notebook and pen, sat down on his bed and wrote as
the voice spoke.

"We are real, Jonathan. We know your
pain and can help you so our message can come
through your heart even while it is in the process
of being purged and cleared. Let the message

133

through and it will do the purging for you.
The message doesn't know how to be distorted
by hurt and pain so it will give you an important vision of the peace and clarity you seek.
Let the vision in. It will lead you and guide you."

Jonathan prepared himself to play this
game out to the end... just to see where
it would lead.

"We are able and very happy to help
ease your planet into the next phase of its evolutionary progression," they went on. "This
is one of the reasons we are here. We are
commissioned to oversee the spiritual integrity
of the universe."

Talk about esteem! Jonathan wondered
about the qualifications you needed to
pull down a job like that.

"When the principles of spiritual unity
which underlie creation are under stress in any
part of the universe, our attentions are called
there much in the same way that white blood
cells in your body are called to muster around
danger zones. It might be useful for you to
think of us as white blood cells in the body
of the universe."

All Jonathan knew for certain was
that all of his emotional pain had
disappeared and he was feeling suddenly joyous.
He wondered if one of the reasons for pain
was so that its disappearance could validate

some inner process like this.

"Our job is to awaken wonder. Wonder is the universe rushing to the rescue of itself, in all things. Our job is to hasten the rescue."

Jonathan was noticing the stirrings of wonder quickening a long-forgotten self.

"Our job is to stir the soup in the cauldron of creation. When life fails to deepen, its substance settles to the bottom of the pot. When the universe was designed, a device was put in to make certain that doesn't happen. That device is who we are. We are the spoon to stir the soup. That we are here is your sign that the spoon is taken in hand by God and the soup is stirred."

Jonathan decided they were probably enlisting him in some clandestine scheme to invade the planet. He was glad to find out they believed in God. He wondered how an invasion would affect the stock market.

"The condition of life on a planet emerges out of a condition of non-life. As life works to establish itself on a planet, non-life pulls back on it, like gravity pulls back on a rocket ship until it breaks free of the pull and enters into free space. Your war arsenals embody that backward pull and proclaim that you have not yet broken free of it. The mentality that produces and maintains your war arsenals embodies that backward pull and proclaims that you have not yet broken free of it. When your war arsenals are dismantled, life will be established on the Earth. This is not yet done... and yet it is accomplished. Destiny speaks because it is already accomplished; otherwise it would not have a voice."

New age. Definitely new age. Jonathan had been warning people for years not to get involved in this kind of thing.

"We are not allowed to interrupt or by our own wills influence the natural progression of any planetary drama... but when communication is established with us by the attunement of your own being, we are permitted to welcome that communication with expressions of good will. Our expressions of good will can be received in many ways. Because they come from what we have learned and become through the course of our own evolutionary schemes, there is much information contained in the information you receive from us and you may unravel those impressions according to your innate capacities as humans. Indeed, the way you unravel them may legitimately influence the course of your affairs on the Earth. That will not be because of our interference but because of your uncovering the common ground between us where we can meet and speak with each other. This is a natural process and one which is held as sacred among all beings in the universe. It is essential for all beings, especially those encamped in the planetary mode, that as they come into the universal consciousness of themselves they establish new contacts on the universal planes of reality. This is another reason we are here.

The voice spoke slowly and consistently as Jonathan wrote. He could feel the voice considering his pace and his psychic capacity.

"Progress upon the path to fulfilling your own natural design, to becoming fully human, produces a spiritual emanation. The dialogue that transpires between your human progression and that spiritual emanation is the focus to secure the next step in your planetary scheme. Tune this dialogue to play in concert with the music that calls together the particles of your creation, the atoms and molecules of your existence. This will bring you to a point where you will be able to gather together as humans with the same closeness that is shared by the members of a molecular aggregate. Until the early unitary particles of materiality started responding to the music of creation, there was no dance to call the particles together and hold them there. The intricate patterns that produce the elemental bodies of your world could not take form until the dance floor was conceived and its call was answered. The same thing holds true for humans as far as creating a universe of humanity is concerned— and it is in your program to encompass the universe. It has been ordained from long before the inception of your world that you will inhabit many planets in many solar systems throughout your galaxy and other galaxies besides.

In your program, humans are the new unitary particles of creation and humanity is the seed of a unique adventure into the realm of density. Your dance has only just begun."

Jonathan listened. His whole body had become an ear that could only listen.

"It is time for civilization to replant its premise——to shift it from the constrictive pot of fear and power into the friable soil of creativity and universal identity. When you cultivate *the creative*, you touch the bonding principles that call together and structure the bodies and forms of existence. When you cultivate *the creative*, you bring the invisible essence of *all being* into worldly visibility. As the qualities of the bonds you form with each other come to simulate more and more closely the qualities of the bonds that call the ocean to the shore and hold it there, your thoughts discover the natural structure of the universe and you become joined, in thought, to the unity of all things."

Jonathan had become a lung that could only breathe...a heart that could only beat.

"The destiny of your race lives in the process you choose for piercing the darkness of dense material...for refining density down to subtlety. A workable process will ease you out onto the dance floor of creation...will refine your bonding potential and make you more accessible to each other as creative units for forming

unions. Unions will greatly ease the stress
which the ensouling spirit of your planet, Gaia,
the vital force of the Earth, is carrying for
you. The burden she is carrying is great and
we have promised her relief. The individual
struggles on your planet of so very many iso-
lated inhabitants for survival serves only to increase the levels of planetary stress which Gaia
is responsible for managing. The first purpose
of the human element on any living planet is to
help the planet's ensouling spirit to keep everything in harmony and balance...and this first purpose is the seed of your relationship to God. Until the first purpose is realized in human life,
the seed is not planted. Until the first purpose
is realized, the seed is hidden in a forgotten
pocket in your soul and not liberated in the garden
of purposeful relationship. If your civilization is
not conceived to under/ine your first purpose,
then this oversight will restrict your natural identity
...and as an unrestricted natural identity is your
legitimate link with *the universal body*, this re-
striction will keep you from claiming the spiritual
inheritance to which you, as a child of creation,
are entitled. Share with each other. Cooperate
with each other. Gather together into committed
forms to facilitate the strategies of sharing and cooperation. You cannot be in profound community with
the Earth when you are not in profound community
with each other. You cannot deal with the life of
the Earth as a whole when you are not dealing
with each other's lives as entireties. Keeping separate from each other keeps you separate from
nature, making yourselves the equivalent of an alien
presence on Earth. Care for the Earth. The first

thing is to do the first thing. This will bring you home to each other. Tune your heart to hear Gaia's plea and your hands will know how to answer."

Jonathan's fingers were tingling with the intensity he was feeling.

"There is great suffering going on all around you, Jonathan. The wounds to which you are subject are deep and harsh and incline you naturally to your own healing. Yet human healing represents a self-centered concern for humans...and self-centered concerns, unless they are balanced by more magnanimous concerns, keep you entrenched in adolescence. Addressing the healing of the individual without addressing the healing of the Earth is forgetting one of the wings of spiritual flight. A healthy presence here and now is one good wing. A world which is whole and at peace with itself is the other one."

Jonathan took a deep breath. The universe filled his lungs. The universe went spilling out. The voice went on.

"Healing is the name of the adventure before you and your race, Jonathan. Hard though it may be to hear the call to adventure through the sting of the wound and the gnaw of the infirmity, the call is there...and responding to it is accepting a great journey. Heal the Earth first, as therein your own healing lies. Heal the Earth and she will expel every infirmity from you and relieve your mind of every unwanted thought."

Jonathan was finding stars alive inside of him. Myriads of stars. His spirit was made of stars.

"Tuning your minds to receive messages from other planes of existence is a part of the evolutionary progression which was programmed into planetary systems when the idea of planetary being was first thought up. So anything that comes as a result of this communication is sanctioned by natural law. This is because it is not we who have come to you but you who have found us. Our rule is to be available. Now that you have found us, we are yours to use as best you can. You may come to us whenever you wish, as there is no distance to cover in coming to this meeting ground. There is neither near nor far in the one being of one life. The spirit that holds the notes together in the song of one moment and the dance of one heart is as immediate as it is immutable."

Jonathan was filled past the limits of his endurance. It was coming to an end.

"So there is no distance between us. It is very important for you to remember this, because your mind grows out of your perceptions and so do your thoughts. Adjusting your thoughts to take the step beyond the idea of distance will help you to move into the heartland of your new reality, where pain is just a voice that isn't being clearly heard or clearly understood.

" **G**o boldly to the truth, Jonathan. **G**oing to the truth is what makes drama and drama is what shows the universe how to unfold in your heart. **T**o go to the truth there needs to be a space to traverse. **T**hings need to be separate from each other. **T**hat separation is an illusion and the spanning of that illusion is the meaning of the interaction going on between us. **A**s in the program it is said that knowing will occur in every heart, even beyond the will, then so moves the hand of creation that in its time not even the blind will be able with blindness to hold back the light.

" **T**he freedom of the mind is in questioning. **T**he freedom of the heart is in answering. **T**he freedom of the soul is in wondering...and wonder heals all things. **Y**et as you cannot live your responsibility to the Earth only partially and survive as a world, you also

THE PRIVILEGE OF ART COMES FROM PROCEEDING WITH KINDNESS. **A**S KINDNESS LINKS THOUGHT WITH THE HANDS AND THE HANDS LINK THOUGHT WITH THE HEART—AS KINDNESS LINKS THE HEART WITH THE WORLD, SO THEN BY KINDNESS ARE ALL THE MEMBERS LINKED IN THE ORDER WHICH SETS THINGS RIGHT AND MAKES ART CERTAIN.

cannot consider the condition of wonder only partially and be healed. **T**he boundaries of your vision determine the capacity of your love ...and love's capacity is the water that keeps wonder's ship afloat. **Y**et nothing will find

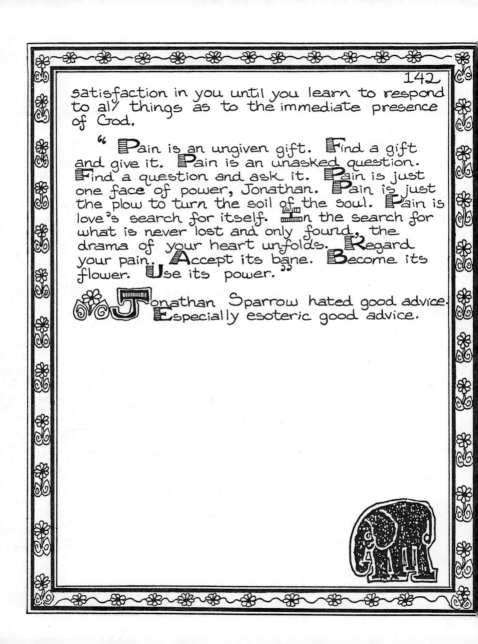

satisfaction in you until you learn to respond to all things as to the immediate presence of God.

" Pain is an ungiven gift. Find a gift and give it. Pain is an unasked question. Find a question and ask it. Pain is just one face of power, Jonathan. Pain is just the plow to turn the soil of the soul. Pain is love's search for itself. In the search for what is never lost and only found, the drama of your heart unfolds. Regard your pain. Accept its bane. Become its flower. Use its power. "

Jonathan Sparrow hated good advice. Especially esoteric good advice.

If the horses are running out of control, head them toward the fire. That will stop them. If there is no fire, call ahead. Have them put one there for you. The nuclear threat is only one fire which we have placed in our own path to force ourselves intently to consider the pace of our horses and to reconsider the concerns of our hearts. We'll reconceive civilization to soften our impact on the earth or leave behind us a grim footprint on the path to eternity.

Rumor has it an irate sibling would have dropped me, a mere babe in arms, off the balcony of our third-floor apartment on Eutaw Place, had not our good grandfather recommended a less direct route to fulfilling my destiny on the Earth.

LADYBUGS

Time spent saving ladybugs, moths and other waterlogged creatures from the chlorinated depths of the Meadowbrook Swimming Pool had me feeling somewhat of a freak. Becoming normal, I was convinced, meant I would have to one day learn how to destroy little lives without conscience or at least learn how to insensibly overlook their sinking below the surface...and growing up has certainly entailed lessons in this regard. Yet try as I might to ignore the little exoskeletal plights plotted by their little navigational blunders, I somehow could never quite learn how to disregard my partnership with them in the world, precluding the possibility of the success of any venture aimed at detaching myself from their lives.

Being inclined, even from my earliest childhood, toward accommodating moral responsibility for lives impounded by delicate circumstances made it seem like a good idea for me to see what I might accomplish by cultivating my natural sensitivities. Going with my resident disposition rather than against it encouraged my trust in the wisdom of the God who was rumored to have designed those kind propensities into the tapestry of my soul. Going *with* my resident disposition rather than against it seemed to quicken my process. It seemed if I could somehow effect the blossoming in my life of who I felt I was naturally, then I could accept my spirit and form from nature's own idea of who it wanted me to be. And as the recommendation of nature seemed best suited to my sensitive condition, I set about the interesting work of learning how to take my natural sensitivities very seriously.

❀ ❀ ❀ ❀

If the instinct to secure personal integrity is actually a modified version of the instinct of the Earth itself toward the continuity of nature, toward securing the integrity of life on the planet...then in the blossoming of personal integrity ❀ ❀ ❀ planetary design is fulfilled in us and the personal instinct finds its best chance to become transformed into the planetary one. Perhaps evolution holds an inheritance in trust for us, planted down among the roots of mindfulness, to be allocated when we come of age, by the cultivation of an instinct ...a planetary instinct...a gentle sense that embraces the whole of it.

The past is the skeleton, the future is the flesh and the present is the workshop where they're thrown all together in one way or another.

ART

Art is a trail left behind
by the future.

Use skies and trees and worms and spiders, shopping sprees and germs and gliders. Love the truth. Take it where you find it. Find it where you give it. Do windows, take shorthand, take dictation and *NEVER* accept collect calls from other worlds without asking what the charges are for the first three minutes. Venture *EVERY* conceivable vulnerability to secure the life of your aspiration, and avoid people who volunteer advice.

Sometimes you think you're making a mistake and it turns out to be art. Sometimes you think you're making art and it turns out to be a mistake. Learning to be comfortable with a medium of art invites art more and more into the medium. Becoming a medium of art invites art more and more into the conduct of our lives, which entails balancing *making things happen* with *letting them happen*...balancing trust with caution... playful abandon with rampaging paranoia. Strategies of healing only uncover the wisdom of art. Art is the eye that opens inward, looking outward ...and the eye that opens outward, looking inward. Art is seeing...really seeing.

Life is the wedding ring in the marriage between body and spirit. The universe is the setting in whose midst the gem is placed. The wonder in your eyes, the love in your heart and the lightness of your step are the three facets in the gem. Joy is the gem.

"What is enlightenment?" the teacher asked. My hand shot up. I didn't know why. She called on me right away.

"Enlightenment is holding up your hand," I said. A whole slew of hands shot up. I lowered mine.

FEARING

FEAR NOTHING BUT THE MEAGERNESS OF YOUR DREAM AND THE DEARTH OF YOUR VISION... THE DREAM THAT STIRS YOU NOT DEEPLY ENOUGH TO QUICKEN THE VITAL ELEMENT OF YOUR SOUL... THE VISION THAT DRAWS YOU NOT GENTLY AND FIRMLY ENOUGH FORWARD TO ITS BREAST WHERE FEAR IS FORGOTTEN IN MOTHER'S MILK. FEAR ONLY THAT WHICH LEAVES YOU DEFICIENT IN SPIRIT. IN DEFICIENCY, PATHOLOGY TAKES HOLD AND HAS ITS WAY WITH US. IN FULLNESS OF SPIRIT, THE MYSTERY OF MYSTERIES STANDS REVEALED IN THE GLIMMER OF OUR EYES AND THE BEATING OF OUR HEARTS.

THE SKY WAS ONCE THE SEA AND THE SEA WAS ONCE THE SKY. THE HORIZON CAME BETWEEN WHEN A QUESTION HAPPENED BY. IT WASN'T VERY MUCH AT FIRST TO OUT OF ONE, MAKE TWO. BUT NOW THE QUESTION'S QUESTION IS THE VESSEL PASSING THROUGH.

Time was invented to make spaces between the words so they don't get garbled when we talk to each other.

THE BULLETiN BOARD

The future is a legitimate part of our psychic bodies.

I was my arrow's flight. I was the fish I caught. There is no random destiny. There is no moment lost. Victory is being unable, no matter how hard you try, to fall from the place where there is no defeat. Love is the victory celebration, the feast of tenderness. Truth is what lives, goodness is what loves; love is the most efficient use of energy. How can we live together in the same world when we haven't learned yet how to live together in the same house? To get a grasp of them, human beings need to be studied at close range.

THE RiDDLE iS AS SiMPLE AS TOMORROW NEVER COMES. TODAY'S ETERNAL PRESENCE KEEPS TOMORROW ON THE RUN. THE RiDDLE OF TOMORROW KEEPS TODAY A STEP AWAY, 'TiL A TALL SHiP DREAMS TOMORROW AND TOMORROW DREAMS TODAY.

Although no one came to me as I had hoped would happen, it was still very interesting how every time I got back to my room after putting something up on the bulletin board outside the coffee shop in the basement of McDowell Hall at St. John's College in Annapolis, Maryland, I thought of a better way to say what I was trying to say. So I would spend the next days running back and forth between my room and the bulletin board changing things and adding things until everybody thought I was crazy, running back and forth so much. But to me it wasn't crazy. To me it seemed I wasn't running at all but was being carried along by a wave sent by *Creation* itself for me to ride as best I could. And feeling myself doing so much what I was doing...and feeling myself *being* so much what I *was*....were very interesting things for me to be feeling. And watching my work grow more full and whole by the touch of my very own hands was a very interesting thing for me to be watching. And by *making* with my hands, it seemed that I was becoming with my heart...and this was a very interesting thing for me to be feeling happening inside of me.

Spirit is an ember, in eternity enduring, waiting to be fanned and fueled to flame. A question is the kindling. Its asking is the fanning. Its answer is the flame.

THE SMALL ROOM
The universe is a detective story...and God is the Watson... to quicken the Holmes in us.

On my way out to Oregon, I met God in a small room on the third floor of a rooming house somewhere in Pittsburgh. It's like there are two sides of sleep and while usually you wake up on the same side you started out from, this time I woke up on the other side and it was all different because the other side is where God lives. It's like falling asleep in a movie theatre and waking up in the projection room with the projectionist right there beside you.

❀

Sister Mary Fidelia taught chemistry at Chatham College in Pittsburgh. She was a member of a small delegation of nuns visiting St. John's to see how *The Great Books Program* worked...as they were thinking of starting a similar program at Chatham. We kept on running into each other.

Facing each other at the top of the steps which she had just ascended and I was about to descend, leading to the coffee shop in the basement of McDowell (after our eleventh or twentieth such interfacing that morning), I considered the possibility of some sort of destiny trying to involve itself in our meeting. We both conceded at the same moment, it seemed, to the skulking determination of whatever design it was that had succeeded in stopping us at last like two trains coming at each other on the same track, screeching to a halt just before colliding. I had never spoken with a nun before. I had no idea what you were supposed to say to one. Having one of my recent writings posted on the bulletin board inside the door at the bottom of the steps, I asked her if she'd like to read something I had written.

"I'd love to," she said...beaming.

There is a spirit indwelling which lays claim to no territory. And as the territory of the heart surrenders itself to no claim, the territory of the heart can only give itself when no claim is made. By giving words the time they need to give themselves to us...by waiting for the words to give themselves rather than forcing them to our will, we speak true and not just paper words...words with hearts. Poised in front of the bulletin board, reading my trembling page, so neatly typed, so vulnerably displayed there for every conceivable type of comment to be planted in every conceivable color of ink in the margins and the spaces between the lines, Sister Mary Fidelia was a tree that gives itself to the woods. Her eyes asparkle, her cheeks aglow, wielding her full black habit like a regal gown, she left me sitting among the ghosts of dialectic passions past, in one of the secluded booths against the wall toward the rear of the coffee shop where Johnnies only sit when they have matters of great importance to discuss. She returned a minute later with two cups of coffee on a tray.

Sister Mary Fidelia pulled from her briefcase a drawing that might easily have been done to illustrate the piece that I had written. In fact, to everything I showed her (I had hurried back to my room and returned with a bundle of my writings), she responded by pulling something more or less appropriate from her briefcase, including some of her own writings. She especially liked a play I had written. She said she had some theatre contacts and would investigate the possibility of getting it produced when she got back to Pittsburgh. She was going to call me on the next weekend to let me know if she had made any progress. The next week was a holiday and I would be at my parents' home in Baltimore so she was going to call me there.

In some orthodox Jewish homes it's traditional secretly to place the telephone receiver up on toothpicks when the youngest son is expecting a long-distance phone call from a Felician nun in Pittsburgh. (Jews protect their children from conversion with a passion. Transformation is kosher. Conversion is not.) The time appointed for her call had passed by half an hour when I noticed the delicate construction concealed beneath the receiver, bridging the parapets on the phone in my parents' bedroom. I erupted out of the house. I ran down to the Dairy Cottage and called Sister Mary Fidelia collect.

On my way out to Oregon seven years later, a local bus dropped me off at the base of a hill just outside the modest business district of Coraopolis, the small town northwest of Pittsburgh whose post office serviced the Felician Sisters. I didn't really expect there to be an airport in the backyard of the convent. I had only toyed with the fantasy of a spiritual whirlwind sweeping me onto a plane and sparing me the pain of hitchhiking the rest of the way to Selma and Paula. But the image of an airport in the backyard of the convent was there in my mind...so the sight of a weather-worn wooden "airport" sign pointing up the steep road leading to the convent spoke in secret to the place inside of me where only secrets are heard. Rising sharply, the road turned and twisted up a lightly wooded hill, up and up until along the left a line of modest white-frame houses appeared. Then the road met the gate of the convent, turned back into a clustering of houses and disappeared.

Like some infinite pain formed in stone, hiding mercifully from memory's probing vision, the convent loomed. Across a patchy lawn dotted with a crowd of pine and spruce, more dirt than grass, I marched. Through a great wooden door, carrying my sleeping bag, knapsack and black velour clothing bag, I entered a dimly lit chamber, cavernous, stone and cold, conspiring with mystery, and was greeted by a lone nun sitting behind a long, heavy oaken counter, attending the switchboard.

I easily convinced myself that my inquiry after Sister Mary Fidelia would be met with the information that she'd left years earlier or there was no such person or I was at the wrong convent, so the sound of the attending nun paging her over the intercom took me by surprise and left me wondering how many Sister Mary Fidelias they had roaming around the place. I was prepared to be met by a stranger so I wasn't surprised when a strange nun appeared at a second great wooden door leading to inner sanctums. We scanned each other's faces for hints of familiarity. I asked her if she was Sister Mary Fidelia, and more as a question than an answer she said "Yes."

As though it were a painting of a great ocean wave that was completely unidentifiable as being a wave until you noticed the form of a tiny surfer courageously negotiating its frothing mountainous slope, the moment defied coherence until I said my name and it was like turning on the lights when no one even knew they were off. She squeezed my hand and took my arm. As we walked through stark and spacious hallways, down a marble staircase and into a large empty cafeteria crowded with long tables and slender cane chairs, I remembered that once during a walk we had taken together on the back campus at St. John's she stopped suddenly, stood off from me, examining me from a distant and curious stance as though she were trying on a new habit and was looking in the mirror to see how it fit...and for some reason which I had decided it was best not to question, said she even liked the way I looked.

Dusk had settled, taking its irreversible hold on the day, and spirit unrelenting passed back and forth across the table where we sat opposite each other. We babbled back and forth in words tempered and animated by mutual regard until signs of my prolonged sleeplessness and eatlessness seemed to capture her attention. She apologized for being unable, due to company policy, to turn her own quarters over to me for the night, gave me the name and address of a friend of hers in Pittsburgh with whom she was confident I'd be able to stay over, then led me back out. Out the cafeteria, up the marble staircase, back through cold glazed hallways, back through one great wooden door and then another one with the nun at the switchboard and the long oaken counter in between, she led me out across the shaggy wooded lawn to the home of an elderly couple across the road, where I was feasted graciously on cookies and milk and crosses and three-dimensional holy pictures on the walls and holy figures on the shelves. Sister Mary Fidelia and the wife waved good-bye as the husband drove off with me in the passenger seat of their old green Chevy pickup. He left me off at the entrance to the expressway heading into Pittsburgh.

Besides the darkness, already fallen, spreading, saturating an evening mist with thoughts of sleep, exhaustion creeping over me like some foggy death, it also turned out that this was a particularly bad spot for hitchhiking. The turnoff entering the expressway was scarcely lit and there was no shoulder for stopping. Cars sped past from around a curve so they couldn't even see me until it was too late to stop and it was too dangerous to stop anyway.

Sometimes you know you've reached the end of the line and you have to either get off of whatever bus you're on and switch over to another one or else sit there and wait for the driver to throw a sheet over you. Sometimes it seems like your death is there in the driver's seat watching you in the mirror. Sometimes watching back, feeling it so close, an almost peaceful temptation sets in to let it have its mournful say even so long before its time, just to get some sleep. In moments like this, even the merest hint of surrender can be enough to prime death's lust to rush and rampage over life's delicate balance. A young couple was coming out of a small diner a short ways back. They were getting into their car when I caught up with them and asked them for help. They left me off in a residential section of Pittsburgh at the address that Sister Mary Fidelia had given to me.

I rang the front doorbell of a large Victorian house across from the campus of some university. It turned out to be a rooming house. The small balding man who answered the door turned out to be the manager.

The person I was looking for wasn't in, he informed me, but he'd be back later on in the evening. He also informed me that the person I was looking for had moved that day from a smaller room on the third-floor to a larger room on the second floor. This left the third-floor room vacant until the next day when a young woman was moving into it...and if I could promise to be out good and early in the morning, I was welcome to it. I left a note on the door of the second-floor room, showered in the common bathroom at the end of the second floor hall, bounced up the stairs, closed the door to the third-floor room, climbed into my sleeping bag, stretched out across a single bed next to the door, looked up at a small window set in a gable on the opposite wall, tucked my black velour clothing bag under my head, and let the anguish of sleeplessness melt away.

Only barely at the threshold of perception, like a placid organ in a hibernating bear, a gentle pulsing mingled with my sleep and changed it into wakefulness. **A** gentle prodding woke me up without intruding on my dreams...woke me up into the dream of dreams. **E**ternity had somehow managed to stuff itself

WHEN THE EYES SEE THE HANDS DOING THE WORK OF THE HEART, THE CIRCLE OF THE SOUL IS CLOSED, THE CIRCLE OF CREATION IS COMPLETED AND THE EYES ARE OPEN AT LAST.

into a tiny room on the third floor of a rooming house somewhere in Pittsburgh and I had somehow managed to wake up in that very room while eternity was still on the premises. **W**hen you wake up with God there in the room with you, there's really no other way to say it except you woke up with God there in the room with you.

I could see the entire celestial anatomy at a single glance, like a multidimensional translucent model of the human body...only God's anatomy doesn't describe material function but profound personality, as God's personality is the anatomy of creation. All the great and small concerns whose constant pursuit makes some things human in their time...every step and stumble along that sacred way and every moment of my own life were all in subtle images and visions displayed there in *The Presence*, as though in every morsel of *The Being* were implanted the entire story of the world. Eternity surrounded and pervaded the little room; it was a sparkling mist, a misty darkness playing lights and hues and shadows like musical instruments changing darkness into sweetness, rich and softly twinkling like dewy moss in the last glimmerings of moonlight. As though I'd just awakened in the deepest, most secret chamber of one of those meandering mazes on the children's puzzle page of the Sunday paper where a hungry puppy waits outside the maze to be guided to her reward by someone with the pencil and the time to spare....as though I'd just traveled through sleep and stumbled across a whole new country on the other side, I opened my eyes for the first time.

What I knew was that I didn't belong there in that room; what I was seeing was for no eye to see. Seeing God profaned God...and if I had *any* respect or *any* sense of decorum, I'd close my eyes as tightly as I could and pray for God to go away. But my eyelids were pinned open. Nothing I could do would make them close. I lay there stupidly gorging my celestial senses on their forbidden object.

It was the sense of God's being embarrassed that took me by surprise...as though it were a great warm snuggly teddy bear that had just swallowed me by mistake with an unexpected *gulp*...and didn't know quite what to do about having me alive and looking around inside its belly. It's not quite right to call it a mistake. It's not quite right to say I didn't belong there in the room with this unexpected visitor.

My first sense of God had been as a peeking through the door...the kind of peeking that a parent does to make sure the children are covered and safe for the night...and I was supposed to be sleeping. I wasn't supposed to be seeing God. But how could I be seeing God if it weren't intended? The apparent contradiction seemed to get resolved in the embarrassment.

You see, it wasn't the usual kind of embarrassment. It wasn't a withdrawal or a hiding from vulnerability but a collaboration with it. The hint of shame wasn't there...and its absence so vastly increased the impact of the vulnerability as to render it, apart from love abounding, God's single most ferocious feature. The visit started as a peeking...then it filled the room.

Guarding vulnerability with greater vulnerability is probing to the roots of reason...is probing to the roots of art and form and joy and pain and art again. **V**ulnerability concealed behind a face of power is a devastation. **G**od's power was to have no power...just a gentle reason tinged with magic...only flickers...tiny sparks and flickers to ignite the kindling wood.

A heart in tune will less easily dismiss the tiniest spark than it will the greatest conflagration. **I**t hadn't been an hour yet since I'd fallen asleep and here I was convinced I'd slept my tired bones away in that short time.

In the center of a magic city is a magic stone. **A**s you ponder on the stone, you're lifted off the ground. **H**igher and higher you go until you have an anxious thought of height or falling, then the spell is broken and down you go. **I**t was such a flight, such a flood and flurry of emotions, that I really couldn't help the anxious stir inside of me. **T**hen God was gone. **T**hen came the knocking on the door. **I**n that very selfsame moment came the knocking. **K**nowing then that it was God, not gone but knocking... **K**nowing it was God there still, though now just past the limits of my sight, just there outside my door, an opening away, and knowing it was me there too...that I was knocking on my door to let me know that I was there with God...and so was Sister Mary Fidelia's second-floor friend knocking on the door to let me know he'd received my note and to invite me to breakfast with him in the morning, fused and one in soaring thought, knowing I would ride a celestial wave...no...*fly* the rest of the way to Oregon, I got up, pulled on my pants and opened the door.

THE MEANING OF CHRISTMAS IS TO CELEBRATE THE CONTINUING BIRTH OF THE UNIVERSE AND THE ETERNAL NEWNESS OF LOVE.

The old
die more
easily when
the young are
happy and the
world secure. There
is an oldness eager to
claim its easy death
but a new field
must first
be cleared
and a new
seed sown.
In
anticipation
of the ripening
grain,
the spirit of the old,
given up more easily
to death, finds
itself alive and new
again in the
harvest when it's due.
In the gift of that
anticipation, the rest
of rests becomes
the dream
of
dreams.

EPILOGUE

Change is imminent. Welcome the imminent. Consort with it as though it were your nearest friend. Nothing is closer to us than the moment of unavoidable experience... and in consorting, nothing teaches better.

FULL CiRCLE

"Nothing can live well except in a manner ❀ ❀ suited to the way the Power of the World lives and moves to do its work."

Black Elk

"You have noticed that everything an Indian does is in a circle and that is because the *Power of the World* always works in circles, and everything tries to be round. In the old days when we were a strong and happy people, all our power came to us from the sacred hoop of the nation, and so long as the hoop was unbroken, the people flourished. The flowering tree was the living center of the hoop and the circle of the four quarters nourished it. The east gave peace and light, the south gave warmth, the west gave rain and the north with its cold and mighty wind gave strength and endurance. This knowledge came to us from the outer world with our

ART iS ALWAYS iNVENTiNG AND REiNVENTiNG iTSELF...AND SO, LiKE LOVE, WE MUST RENEW OUR COMMITMENT TO iT FROM ONE MOMENT TO THE NEXT (JUST TO KEEP UP WiTH iT) UNTiL ALL THE MOMENTS FUSE TOGETHER iNTO ONE.

religion. Everything the Power of the World does is done in a circle. The sky is round, and I have heard that the Earth is round like a ball and so are all the stars. The wind, in its greatest power, whirls. Birds make their nests in circles, for theirs is the same religion as ours. The sun comes forth and goes down again in a circle. The moon does the same, and both are round.

"Even the seasons form a great circle in their changing, and always come back again to where they were. The life of a man is a circle from childhood to childhood, and so it is in everything where power moves. Our tepees were round like the nests of birds and these were always set in a circle, the nation's hoop, a nest of many nests, where the *Great Spirit* meant for us to hatch our children."

Black Elk

❀   ❀   ❀   ❀

When Black Elk was a child, he had a vision of circles and circles of circles, the nation of many hoops stretching across the plains for as far as the eyes could see. With dance, in chants, with song and verse, he showed his vision to his tribe. He prepared himself and when he was ready, he stood before his tribe, the *Oglala Sioux*, and gave life to what stirred in his heart and moved in his blood. Until his vision was performed for his people, it had no power. To give power to a vision, it must be performed for the people. Now I also, like Black Elk, have performed my vision for you, my tribe, to give it power.

❀   ❀   ❀   ❀

The silence embraces our thoughts like an ocean embraces the hull of a sailing ship. When our thoughts are true, when they have no holes in them, they stay afloat. When they have oars, we can go for a ride in them. When they are big enough, we can take some friends along. When they come from the heart, a great adventure is at hand.

NOTE TO THE READER
    Needless to say, Michael is very serious about the vision contained in these pages — and about finding answers to the questions that it raises. He is anxious to communicate with people who are ready to discuss related issues. He can be reached through *Times Change Press*, P.O. Box 1380, Ojai, California 93024.

It's nice finding people who are going to the same place you are. It gives you something to talk about in the car.

POSTSCRIPT

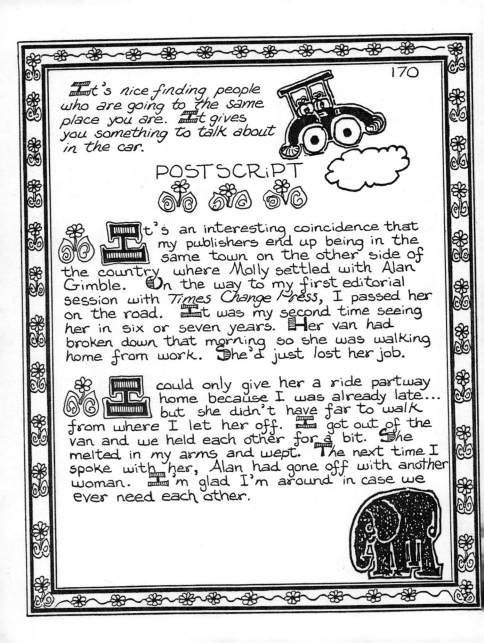

It's an interesting coincidence that my publishers end up being in the same town on the other side of the country where Molly settled with Alan Gimble. On the way to my first editorial session with *Times Change Press*, I passed her on the road. It was my second time seeing her in six or seven years. Her van had broken down that morning so she was walking home from work. She'd just lost her job.

I could only give her a ride partway home because I was already late.... but she didn't have far to walk from where I let her off. I got out of the van and we held each other for a bit. She melted in my arms and wept. The next time I spoke with her, Alan had gone off with another woman. I'm glad I'm around in case we ever need each other.